TO:

....

FROM:

....

DATE:

....

DEVOTIONS FOR A

"Moving Mountains"

Kind of Girl

DEVOTIONS FOR A

"Moving Mountains"

Kind of Girl

INSPIRATION & ENCOURAGEMENT
FOR TEENS

JANICE THOMPSON

BARBOUR
PUBLISHING

Mountain Mover

*"You don't have enough faith," Jesus told them. "I tell you
the truth, if you had faith even as small as a mustard seed,
you could say to this mountain, 'Move from here to there,'
and it would move. Nothing would be impossible."*

Matthew 17:20 nlt

You can have the kind of faith that moves mountains. It's true!

Maybe you read that and think, *Not me! My faith is so small I can barely
find it most days.* Welcome to the club! Most people would say the same thing.
But God says we don't need much. Just a tiny bit is all it takes to speak to
mountains and watch them move.

What mountains are you facing in your life right now? Anxiety? Doubt?
Depression? Loneliness? Insecurity? Look them in the eye and speak to them
in the name of Jesus; then watch them disappear!

The 180 devotions you find in this book will help you face those mountains. You will learn to face your challenges with the kind of faith that gets
things done. Best of all, you'll discover that everything *doesn't* depend on
you. Jesus is right there, and it's His power that lives inside of you.

What are you waiting for, girl? It's time to move some mountains!

Why Did You Doubt Me?

Jesus immediately reached out and grabbed him.
"You have so little faith," Jesus said. "Why did you doubt me?"
MATTHEW 14:31 NLT

Have you ever doubted someone? Maybe you put your trust in a friend. She said she'd be there for you, but when it really counted. . .she wasn't. It's easy to be disappointed by people, isn't it?

Here's a fact: Jesus will never disappoint you. He's a follow-through sort of friend. So when He says, "I'll be there for you," He really means it. And if He means it (and proves it time and time again, no matter what awful stuff you're going through), then you can trust Him.

What does it mean to trust God? First, you can take a deep breath because He's not only aware of your situation—He's also on top of it. Second, you can throw away your worries and doubts. You don't have to wonder, *Is He really paying attention? Does He care?* He is. . .and He does. In fact, He cares ten thousand times more than even you do, girl!

Sure, you're facing mountains. They look insurmountable, way too big for you to handle. And honestly? They are. By yourself. . .you can't. But with Him. . .you can. Actually, *He* can. You'll just be a witness to the miracle when it takes place.

Put your trust in Him. Toss those doubts to the curb. He's never failed you before, and He's not going to start now!

⤜⟶

I feel like I've been disappointed so many times, Jesus. Over and over again, people have let me down. But I'm safe with You.

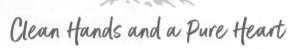

Clean Hands and a Pure Heart

*I desire therefore that the men pray everywhere, lifting
up holy hands, without wrath and doubting.*
1 TIMOTHY 2:8 NKJV

It's easy to go into a church service and sing your heart out, hands lifted high, praising God. Worshipping Him brings joy to His heart. But you know what makes Jesus even happier? When you worship Him with clean hands and a pure heart.

Maybe you wonder why you can worship on Sunday and face so many trials on Monday. (Part of that is just the result of living in a fallen world.) But it might also be that you have some issues in your life that you're not dealing with six days of the week. You're expecting one worship service to fix everything.

Girl, deal with the stuff. If there's sin in your life, get rid of it. If you're angry with someone, forgive them and get past it. If you're struggling with an ugly secret, voice it to God. He can handle it.

Here's the point: lift holy hands—without wrath (anger) or doubting. You'll have an easier time getting rid of doubt when you've taken care of the icky stuff. And when you do, those mountains in your life? They have to move!

---

*It's not easy, Jesus, but I'm coming to You today with the hidden
stuff. I know You see it anyway. I ask for forgiveness and healing
so that doubt can dissolve and mountains can move. Amen.*

When Doubt Fills Your Mind. . .

*When doubts filled my mind, your comfort
gave me renewed hope and cheer.*
PSALM 94:19 NLT

Have you ever felt like your mind was so full that you couldn't squeeze in one more thing? Maybe you've had a long week at school—filled with crazy classes, tests, or relational issues. Then along comes a problem. A big one. One that feels like a mountain taller than Mount Everest.

And you're done. You're totally and completely done. No one can convince you to lay down your doubts. You don't have the energy. You don't have the desire to have faith. You're just. . .over it.

Take a look at today's verse. The psalmist says, "When doubts filled my mind. . ."

Stop to think about that. You know that feeling well. You've been full of doubt that even pretending to have faith felt impossible. But it was there, in that super low place, that the writer of today's psalm gave us the God-answer: "Your comfort gave me renewed hope and cheer."

Think about it. You're done. You're over it. But that's exactly when God plans to show up and show off! That way you won't be tempted to take the credit for it!

No matter how low you are—no matter how bad your day (or week or month) has been—you don't have to lose hope. Sure, you're riddled with doubt. But Jesus isn't. And He's right there beside you, ready to sweep into action!

⟫⟫⟶

I trust You, Jesus. Especially now, when I'm over it! Thank You in advance for the comfort and hope You're bringing. I'm ready! Amen.

If You Have Faith

Then Jesus told them, "I tell you the truth, if you have faith
and don't doubt, you can do things like this and much
more. You can even say to this mountain, 'May you be
lifted up and thrown into the sea,' and it will happen."
MATTHEW 21:21 NLT

The story of your faith in Jesus really can be summed up in today's verse. Jesus told His followers, "If you have faith and don't doubt, then you can do miraculous things."

Let's stop right there. Maybe you've never considered the fact that God could use you to perform miracles. That sounds like something that only happened to people in Bible days.

The truth is, God can and will perform the miraculous on your behalf, if you have faith and if you don't doubt. So your journey begins by placing your trust in Him.

Now look at the rest of that verse. You can say to a mountain, "May you be lifted up and thrown into the sea," and it will happen.

Whoa. That seems pretty extreme. . .until you realize the kind of mountains He's talking about. Anger is a mountain. So is jealousy. So is grief. And pain. And unforgiveness. You'll face a lot of mountains in this life, but Jesus wants you to know that if you don't doubt, they will have to go when you say so! Speak to your loneliness in the name of Jesus. Speak to your frustrations, your pain. Poof! Away they will go at the mention of His name!

Today I speak to the mountains in my life. You have to go, in
Jesus' name! Thank You, Lord, for reminding me that with
Your help, I'm capable of moving mountains. Amen.

Doubt-Free Living

"Why are you frightened?" he asked.
"Why are your hearts filled with doubt?"
LUKE 24:38 NLT

You were created by God to be doubt-free. Read that again. You're created in His image—in the image of the one true and holy God. And He never doubts. (Hey, He knows what's coming, so He's totally chill!)

If you're really created in His image (and you are), then you've got to learn to let go of doubts too. You can trust Him. You really can.

Here's where it gets tricky: Sometimes you put your trust in people and they let you down. As a result, a lot of your doubts have to do with those people. You were never meant to put your trust in them, girl. But you can always trust the Lord—with the big stuff and the small stuff.

That test you're worried about? Trust Him. Don't doubt that He can give you the knowledge and peace to get through it. That health crisis your loved one is facing? God is big enough to handle that too.

"Why are you frightened?" That's what Jesus asked His disciples. "Why are your hearts filled with doubt?" He was really just saying, "I've got this, people!" And even though two thousand years have passed. . .He's still got this.

───────►

You've still got this, Jesus. Time has passed, but You're still the same miracle-working God as always. How could I ever doubt You? Amen.

What Are You Leaning On?

He said to Thomas, "Put your finger into My hands.
Put your hand into My side. Do not doubt, believe!"
JOHN 20:27 NLV

Imagine you've been asked to paint a house. You have a tall ladder (and good thing too because it's a two-story house). Now imagine you take that ladder and, instead of leaning it against the house, you choose to lean it against a rickety old fence nearby. What's going to happen? You'll fall, of course, because a ladder is only as good as what you're leaning it against.

The same is true with your faith. If you lean the ladder of faith against disbelief (or doubts), you'll fall every time.

One man who found this out the hard way was Thomas, one of Jesus' disciples. He's known as "Thomas the Doubter," or "Doubting Thomas." Even when he saw that Jesus had (clearly!) been raised from the dead, he thought his eyes were deceiving him. He asked for proof. He wanted to feel the wounds in Jesus' hands to prove he had the right guy!

Don't be a doubting Thomas. Lean your ladder against your beliefs, not your doubts.

I don't want to be a doubting Thomas, Lord. I put my faith and
my trust in You. You'll keep me standing strong! Amen.

Your Words Are Powerful

"The Holy Spirit told me to go with them and not doubt about going. These six men also went with me to this man's house."
ACTS 11:12 NLV

You've been told that you can move mountains. You're not so sure. And it shows, girl. The things you say. . .the things you do. They're a reflection of your doubts, not your faith.

Why do you suppose it matters so much what you say, anyway? Who cares if you speak in faith?

Think about it this way: if Jesus took the time to say, "Speak to the mountain," then your words must be very powerful. They're also a reflection of your trust in Him. But those same powerful words can be used in a negative way if you're not careful.

Complaining. Whining. Gossiping. These are all examples of ways your powerful words can work against you.

Here's the truth: your words are working. They're active. They're powerful. Are you using them for you or against you?

The choice is up to you.

→

I get it, Jesus. My words are powerful. They carry a lot of weight.
And, I confess, I've been using them in a not-so-great way at times.
Help me to stay focused on using those powerful words for good! Amen.

A Wave Pushed Around by the Sea

You must have faith as you ask Him. You must not doubt.
Anyone who doubts is like a wave which is pushed around by the sea.
JAMES 1:6 NLV

Anyone who doubts is like a wave pushed around by the sea.

What images come to mind when you read that phrase? Maybe you see a lonely inner tube floating on the water at the beach. It's being pushed in and out by the waves, almost making it to shore at times but then being pushed back out by the stronger waves.

Maybe you see yourself, struggling in hard seasons. The waves of life are coming at you hard and fast. They pull you toward shore, and you start to feel safe. Then they drag you back out to the depths again, and you fear you might drown.

Life is hard, girl. And there are plenty of moments when you might doubt God's faithfulness. But He's always going to bring you back to shore. He won't let you drown. That's a promise. (And God never breaks His promises.)

Don't doubt, even when the waves are crashing around you. You'll land on the shore soon enough!

I won't give in to doubt, even when the waves are pounding
me, Lord. When I feel like I've lost control. When fear
kicks in. Even then, I won't doubt You, Jesus! Thank You
for taking care of me in good times and bad. Amen.

He Loves Me!

Have loving-kindness for those who doubt.
JUDE 1:22 NLV

"He loves me, he loves me not." That's a silly little game that girls used to play, plucking petals off flowers in a field. If you got to the last petal on "He loves me!" you took that to mean, well, he loved you!

Here's the cool thing about God—you don't need flower petals to discern His love. He loves you—no matter what—even on days when you're not feeling very lovable. He continues to pour out His loving-kindness, regardless of your feelings on the matter.

And here's the thing—He wants you to continue to pour it out too. This can be especially tough with certain people in your world. They're like mountains (or obstacles) in your path. But God has loving-kindness for you even when you doubt. So why would you withhold loving-kindness from others when they're being testy?

You don't have that right, girl. Love keeps on giving, even when it doesn't feel like it. In fact, that's the most beautiful love of all—the kind that gives itself away to one who doesn't deserve it. Isn't that what Jesus did when He died on the cross, after all?

You love me, Jesus! And You're showing me how to love others, even when I feel they don't deserve it. Thank You for Your loving-kindness! Amen.

Wisdom Is Pure

*But the wisdom that comes from heaven is first of all pure.
Then it gives peace. It is gentle and willing to obey. It is
full of loving-kindness and of doing good. It has no doubts
and does not pretend to be something it is not.*

JAMES 3:17 NLV

Can we pause for a minute to talk about the "wisdom is pure" part of today's verse? Maybe you feel like your wisdom-meter is running low. You're making some not-so-great choices and the fallout is real. You're now facing mountains that rose up simply because of your own choices.

And you're thinking to yourself, *I'm better than this. I'm smarter than this. How did I get into this mess, anyway?*

True wisdom doesn't have a lot to do with book smarts. It's something that streams straight down from God. And you can ask for more. If you're starting to feel depleted and your life choices are reflecting that, just pray this simple prayer: "Lord, I need Your wisdom, not my own." The Spirit of God will infuse you with it! You'll be like a car with gas in the tank.

You'll make better choices and face fewer mountains with a megadose of godly wisdom. It's yours! Just ask for it.

---

*Lord, today I come to You asking for Your wisdom. I've tried
doing things my way, but that has gotten me nowhere. I need
the wisdom only You can give. Fill my tank, please! Amen.*

Overcoming Unbelief

*Immediately the boy's father exclaimed, "I do
believe; help me overcome my unbelief!"*
MARK 9:24 NIV

Here's a little backstory on today's Bible verse. A man brought his son to Jesus. The poor boy had been having attacks all his life—fit-like episodes where he would go rigid and foam at the mouth. (Poor kid, right?)

The dad was over it. He wanted his boy healed. So he brought him to Jesus. He had already taken the boy to the disciples (Jesus' followers) but they couldn't heal him, so they came straight to the Savior. (That's a great lesson, by the way! Go straight to Jesus when you have a problem!)

The man had already been disappointed once before, so when he got to Jesus, he said, "I believe. . .but help me in my unbelief." In other words, "I want to take You at Your word, but I've been hurt in the past. I still have doubts."

You've probably felt that way! But here's the good news: when you go straight to the source, He will move in miraculous ways and prove, once and for all, that there's no reason to ever doubt Him.

⟫⟫⟫———————→

*I've been there so many times, Jesus! I want to believe,
and yet I'm stuck in my doubts. I'll come straight to
You. Help me in my unbelief, I pray. Amen.*

Time to Let Go

What do people get for all the toil and anxious
striving with which they labor under the sun?
ECCLESIASTES 2:22 NIV

One of the largest mountains you'll ever face is the mountain of anxiety. Maybe it starts out small—like tiny pebbles. Little irritations that start to get to you. Then bigger issues start piling up. They're like rocks the size of eggs. Only, you're still anxious about the tiny pebbles. Then boulder-sized problems come and you're completely overwhelmed. Why? Because you didn't take the time to release the smaller issues you were facing yesterday.

Things pile up if you're not careful. Before long you're staring at a mountain of solid rock and thinking to yourself, *How did I get here? And how do I get past all these anxieties?* They hold you locked in place, like a prizefighter pinning you down in the ring.

There's really only one way to rid yourself of anxiety and stress. You have to hand that stuff over to Jesus. You have to picture yourself releasing the problems from your own hands and putting them into His.

Do you see Him standing in front of you now? His hands are outstretched. His palms are open. He's ready, willing, and able to hold mountains in His hands.

What are you waiting for? It's time to let go, girl.

I'm so tired of being stressed out, Jesus! It's like a massive
mountain in front of me and I'm over it! I'm done!
So today I choose to pass this mountain off to You.
I'm so glad You can handle it, because I sure can't! Amen.

Anxiety Is Not Your Friend, Girl!

*Be anxious for nothing, but in everything by prayer and
supplication, with thanksgiving, let your requests be made known
to God; and the peace of God, which surpasses all understanding,
will guard your hearts and minds through Christ Jesus.*

PHILIPPIANS 4:6–7 NKJV

Did you know that anxiety can make you sick? It's true! One minute you're worked up about something, and the next minute you've got a headache or sick stomach. One minute you're going ballistic over a problem at school, and the next minute you're in bed with the covers over your head, feeling like you can't function anymore.

Stress weighs you down. It's like a backpack that's overloaded with books. And it's no fun to drag around something like that, especially when it's so unnecessary.

Jesus tells His mountain-moving girls: "Be anxious for nothing." And, well, nothing means nothing. So you can't get worked up about your grades, your parents, your kid sister, your messy room, or even that BFF who's annoying you. Sure, you'll have moments of irritation, but sometimes you blow them up into something huge. (C'mon, you know you do that from time to time. . .admit it!)

Make small deals out of things, not big ones. Really, the one who will benefit most. . .is you. You're guarding your health when you don't overreact. And besides, God promises to give you peace if you just trust Him. It is possible, you know!

———————⟶

*I'll put my trust in You instead of blowing up, Jesus. I know I'll be better
off in the long run, anyway! Help me in the moment, I pray. Amen.*

Searching the Deep Places

*Search me, God, and know my heart; test me
and know my anxious thoughts.*
PSALM 139:23 NIV

Have you ever known anyone who had their home raided by the police? When those officers enter the home, they're relentless! They won't stop until they've found what they're looking for. They open every drawer, look under every bed, and snoop in every medicine cabinet. They leave no stone unturned.

In some ways, God is like that. When you say, "Lord, come and search my heart—see if there's any anxious thing in me," He does! Oh boy, does He! He looks in the secret, hidden crevices and sees things you've probably forgotten about—the pain from that breakup with your best friend. The anger toward your dad who abandoned your family. The grief from the loss of your favorite grandparent.

God not only sees; He's ready to heal you. Those mountains that have weighed you down (even the things you'd forgotten about) can be lifted with ease by a heavenly Father who wants to see you walking in freedom.

Let Him search the deep places today. Sure, things might get uncomfortable for a little while, but if you allow Him to root out the tough stuff, you can walk in total freedom, girl.

---

*Lord Jesus, sweep in and heal me! Do the work. Root out the pain,
the grief, the unforgiveness, the anxiety. Move those oppressive
mountains out of the way so that freedom can come. Amen.*

You Were Chosen

*Dear friends, God the Father chose you long ago and knew
you would become his children. And the Holy Spirit has been
at work in your hearts, cleansing you with the blood of Jesus
Christ and making you to please him. May God bless you richly
and grant you increasing freedom from all anxiety and fear.*

1 PETER 1:2 TLB

Do you know someone who's been adopted? (Maybe you're pointing to yourself right now!)

When a child is adopted, the new parents deliberately choose him or her. Think about that: kiddos who are born naturally to a family are there by God's choice, but a family that "picks" an adopted child plays a larger role in the choosing.

Here's a fun fact: God chose you. Long before you were born, He went over a list of people He would pursue and you made the list. He knew you would be His. Reflect on that truth for a moment. Before you said yes to Jesus, He knew you would become His child. (How did He know you would say yes?)

The Spirit of God has been working in you all along. Does knowing that bring you great joy? You were chosen! You're His kid. And He cares so much about you. He wants you to be set free from the things that bug you—including the stress you carry from day to day.

He picked you. And as a daughter of the King, you can experience freedom from anxiety and fear. Tell those mountains they have to go, in Jesus' name!

*I'm so honored and humbled that You chose me, Jesus.
I'm Your child! Thank You for caring enough to set me free
from the things that had me so stressed out and fearful. Amen.*

He Will Do It

"Therefore I tell you, do not be anxious about your life, what you will eat or what you will drink, nor about your body, what you will put on. Is not life more than food, and the body more than clothing?"
MATTHEW 6:25 ESV

Have you ever grown anxious, wondering if God was going to come through for you? Maybe you've watched your parents struggle with finances. They've worried that they might not have the money to buy groceries. Or pay the mortgage. Or cover the car payment.

These are real struggles that people face, real mountains that rise up from time to time.

During the hard seasons, it's so good to be reminded that God not only cares but also promises to give you everything you need. Those mountains disappear with just a word from Him. He can put food on the table. He can cover the price tag for that school event you need to attend. He can even put together a plan for the college you'll be going to.

In short, He's got this. So don't be anxious about it at all. If God feeds the birds of the air, what makes you think He won't take care of the details of your life? He will, girl. He will.

I can trust You to come through for me, Lord, so I'll lay my worries aside. You see the areas where I'm struggling. You see the things I'm lacking. And You've already worked out a plan, so I won't worry! I'll just keep on trusting You, even when I can't see it. Amen.

A Tree by the Waters

*"For he shall be like a tree planted by the waters,
which spreads out its roots by the river, and will not fear
when heat comes; but its leaf will be green, and will not be
anxious in the year of drought, nor will cease from yielding fruit."*
JEREMIAH 17:8 NKJV

Picture a large oak tree in your front yard. The roots are visible above the ground. In fact, you trip over them while running across the grass.

The roots of a large tree spread in every direction. The older a tree gets, the larger its root system becomes. And when a huge storm blows in, the only reason that tree refuses to topple is because those roots are clinging with great force to the ground below.

When you're walking with Jesus—really walking deep with Him—you develop a root system like that. The more time you spend with Him, the deeper your spiritual roots go. And when life throws storms your way, you'll stay upright, no matter what. You won't topple. You'll barely feel the winds, in fact.

If you're struggling in your faith right now, just spend time with Him. More and more and more.

*I'll spend more time with You, Jesus! I want to be like a
tree planted by the waters with deep, deep roots that
lead straight to You! Help me, I pray. Amen.*

A Kind Word

Anxiety weighs down the heart, but a kind word cheers it up.
Proverbs 12:25 niv

Imagine you're on a trek across the desert and you've been tasked with carrying a large backpack filled with supplies. It's weighing you down, causing you to walk more slowly. The weight is almost more than you can bear, and you find yourself falling again and again.

Then along comes a guide. He reaches out, grabs the heavy pack, and slings it over his own shoulders. Off he goes, whistling a happy tune and walking with ease.

This might seem like a silly example, but that's kind of how it is when you give your anxieties to the Lord. They've been weighing you down for ages now. They've risen up in front of you like gargantuan, immovable mountains. Then along comes Jesus! With a fingertip He reaches for those anxieties, scooping them up as if they weigh nothing at all.

Only, of course, they did weigh something. He carried the weight of your pain all the way to the cross, where He paid the ultimate price so that you could be set free.

Walk in freedom, girl! Let go of those things that
are weighing you down. Give them to Him, once
and for all, so that you can walk in peace.
I'm giving my worries and my strivings to You, Jesus.
They've been weighing on me, and I'm ready to be rid of
them. Thank You for carrying them for me! Amen.

His Great Comfort

When anxiety was great within me, your consolation brought me joy.
PSALM 94:19 NIV

Often a baby will begin crying in the wee hours of the night. Picture the mother—exhausted after watching over the baby all day, and finally in her bed. She hears the cries, pushes back the covers, and stands to her feet. Then she makes her way across the dark room and out into the hallway, taking careful steps toward the baby's room.

Once she arrives, she reaches down into the crib and picks up her little one, then soothes him with words of comfort, consolation, and love. It takes a minute for his sobs to still, but eventually he stops crying and falls back asleep. Her nearness puts him at such ease that he's finally able to rest.

The same is true when God tiptoes into your situation. Even if you've been in meltdown mode, His mere presence can change everything. His words of comfort and consolation bring great joy, right there in the middle of your pain.

He's a mountain-moving God and He's longing to comfort you today, no matter what you're walking through. Will you let Him?

>>>>————————>

Lord, I'll let You! I need Your comfort and peace.
Anxiety has been tearing me up, and I'm so over it!
Sweep in and bring comfort, I pray. Amen.

Working Hard. . .for What?

So what do people get in this life for all their hard work and anxiety?
ECCLESIASTES 2:22 NLT

Some people work long days—ten or even twelve hours a day. They slave away, and all for a paycheck.

But what if you worked and worked, only to get to the end of the pay period with a message from your boss: "Change of plan! You're not getting paid for all that work." You would be really angry, right? Who works for free?

In some ways, living with anxiety is like working for a paycheck that never comes. You slave away every day, trying to stay on top of things. You work, work, work, often pouring your energies into things that don't really matter (what some people would call noneternal things). In the end, you're exhausted and you haven't made much progress.

If you're worn out, make absolutely sure the things you're pouring yourself into are God things. Ask Him, "Lord, is this Your absolute best for me? Am I supposed to be doing this?"

Sometimes we forget to ask those important questions and pay a heavy price for getting involved in things that were never ours to tackle in the first place!

Lord, I'm so busy! Sometimes it feels like I'm drowning in work and activities. Show me the things You have for me. . .and only those things! I want to lay everything else down. Amen.

Say the Words

*Say to those who have an anxious heart, "Be strong;
fear not! Behold, your God will come with vengeance,
with the recompense of God. He will come and save you."*
ISAIAH 35:4 ESV

"Say to those who have an anxious heart. . ."

Look at those words and ponder them. When you see someone with an anxious heart, how do you usually respond? Most of us turn in the opposite direction. We don't want to speak, for fear we'll make the situation even worse than it already is.

But the same God who has told us to "speak to the mountain" is telling us in this verse that we are to speak—aloud—to those who are anxious. Why? Because these worked-up people are facing mountains of their own. And they need to know there is hope for their situation.

God tells us to speak our faith aloud. . .a lot! The Bible is filled with verses like this. There's something so powerful about the spoken word.

So speak up. When your friend, your sister, your mom, your neighbor, or that girl who sits next to you in science class is struggling, say these words: "Be strong! Don't be afraid. God is going to show up and show off in your situation. He's going to sweep in and save you!"

If you actually say something like that (in your own words, of course), the Lord can use you to lift the spirits of the person who's hurting and help turn their attitude (and maybe even their situation) around.

*Give me the courage to speak words of faith to those
who are struggling, Jesus! I need courage to help others
see You as a mountain-moving God! Amen.*

Whose Desires Are You Chasing?

You won't spend the rest of your lives chasing your own desires, but you will be anxious to do the will of God.
1 PETER 4:2 NLT

What does it mean to chase your own desires? Maybe you want to make the cheer squad. You practice, audition. . .and don't make it. Or maybe you're dying to try out for a part in the school musical. So, you work your hardest and land in the chorus. Or you set your sights on the top college but get a disappointing rejection letter.

What's up with that? Don't your dreams matter? Doesn't God see the desires of your heart?

It's fun to chase after dreams, and life will give you plenty of opportunities to do so. But at some point, you'll figure out that some of those so-called dreams don't pan out, especially if they're not God's dreams for you. In fact, some of the mountains you'll face in life will rise up as a result of chasing after things that were never meant to be yours.

It's so important to know Jesus intimately so that You can hear His still, small voice about these things. Follow hard after Him. In fact, chase only after Him and He'll surprise you by giving you the things you're really meant to have in your life. And when you're walking that closely with Him, you'll scale any mountains together.

I want to follow hard after You, Jesus. Sure, I have lots of dreams. I want to do so much with my life! But I want to be on the right path. I know You can take me there, so I will trust You. Amen.

Don't Be Afraid of Them

*"Be strong and courageous. Do not fear or be in dread
of them, for it is the L*ORD *your God who goes with
you. He will not leave you or forsake you."*
DEUTERONOMY 31:6 ESV

Do not fear or be in dread of them.

So who is "them"? It could be anyone who's risen up against you, right? Maybe yesterday's "them" is different from today's "them." Maybe you've already courageously faced the "thems" from your past, but new ones have risen up.

Here's the thing: you've made it through tough times before. Many times. And the things you're facing now—the people and the situations—might look intimidating, but they're no more powerful than what you've already overcome.

God will help you again. He won't leave you or forsake you. (Has He ever? Um, no!) So stand strong. Be courageous. When God says, "Don't be scared of them," He really means it. With His help, you can say no to fear, refusing to let it rise up and consume you.

He's got this. He's always had this.

Let Him do it again, girl.

---

*I don't know why I get so knotted up with fear, Jesus.
Am I forgetful? Why don't I seem to remember all the times
You've come through for me in the past? I know You'll do it
again. You've been faithful in every situation. So today I'm
choosing not to be afraid of the "thems" in my life. Amen.*

Wherever You Go

"Have I not commanded you? Be strong and courageous. Do not be frightened, and do not be dismayed, for the Lord your God is with you wherever you go."

JOSHUA 1:9 ESV

Picture a family that lives in one part of the country, then moves to another part of the country. Maybe the dad (or mom) is in the military and they have no choice but to relocate a lot. Maybe they've even lived overseas for a season. It must be hard, jumping from place to place, school to school, friends to friends.

Now think about that in light of today's verse. God is with you. . .wherever you go. That doesn't just mean right here and right now either. It means tomorrow. And next month. And next year. And ten—or twenty or thirty—years from now.

Always and forever, God is with you. No matter where you live. No matter which school you attend. No matter which friends hang around and which ones don't. Even if you move to Montana. Or New York. Or Texas. (Crazy to think He's everywhere, right? But He is!)

Is it getting easier to see why you don't need to be frightened? If the Lord is capable of sticking with you wherever you go, then He is big enough to move the mountains you face along the way.

Thanks for sticking with me, Lord. You've always been right here, Jesus. I'm so grateful! Amen.

Don't Let Them Stop You!

And Joshua said to them, "Do not be afraid or dismayed;
be strong and courageous. For thus the Lord will do
to all your enemies against whom you fight."
JOSHUA 10:25 ESV

Do you have enemies in your life? Are there people who seem to be dead set against you, always hoping you'll fail? Do they trip you up or turn on you? If so, you're in good company!

The Bible is filled with stories of heroes of the faith who had enemies. David had Goliath. Moses had Pharaoh. Samson had the Philistines. Elijah had Jezebel. The disciples had the religious leaders. Even Jesus had to do battle against the Pharisees and Sadducees, who wanted to see Him—and His message—stopped.

There will always be people trying to stop you. But if Jesus could stand up to the ones who opposed His message, so can you. If Moses could stand up to Pharaoh and lead the Israelites to the Promised Land, think of what God can do through you.

These people are like mountains in your way at times. But your mountain-moving God can clear the road ahead of you. Like David, Moses, the disciples, and all the great men and women of faith, you can overcome and do great things for the Lord.

I won't let my enemies get me down, Jesus! I have read
the stories in the Bible. I know that good triumphs over evil!
I know that You are the one who really fights our battles for
us. Clear a path. Make it smooth. Move my enemies out of the
way so that I'm free to do all You've called me to do. Amen.

I'm Just Not Feeling It. . . .

*"But you, take courage! Do not let your hands be
weak, for your work shall be rewarded."*
2 Chronicles 15:7 esv

"I just don't feel like it."

How many times have you said those words? There are days when you're just done. You can't. You don't have it in you. You're worn out, run down, and ready to quit.

That's exactly when God is able to step in. He can give you the courage and the energy to keep going, even when it feels physically, emotionally, and psychologically impossible.

You will feel weak at times, but He can make you strong. You will be tired, but He can energize you. You will want to run away from your problems, but He will give you the courage to face them head-on, to speak to them boldly in the name of Jesus. And you know what happens when you speak to something in the name of Jesus, right? It has to flee!

Don't give up. Don't give in. Ask for His strength today, and then watch as He fills you up to overflowing!

*I'll admit it, Jesus! I'm just not feeling it some days. It would
be easier to give up, to quit, to pull the covers over my head.
But Your Word says my work will be rewarded if I don't give up,
so here I am, saying, "Help!" I can only keep going if You give
me the strength, so that's what I'm asking for today. Amen.*

Don't Be Scared of the Horde

"Be strong and courageous. Do not be afraid or dismayed before the king of Assyria and all the horde that is with him, for there are more with us than with him."

2 CHRONICLES 32:7 ESV

Take a look at the verse above. Do you know what the word *horde* means? A horde is a large group of people. In this particular case, it was a large group of people who stood in opposition to the person who wrote this verse!

Maybe you've had a "horde" against you at times too. Maybe a group of girls ganged up against you, or maybe your siblings formed a clique and left you out. It's hard to be the one everyone ignores. Or worse. . .the one everyone torments.

When these things happen—and they will—remember, God is for you, not against you. So be strong in Him. Don't let the horde get you down. They'll pick a new person to mess with tomorrow. Or the next day. In the meantime, don't ever feel alone. You aren't. God can give you courage to hold your head up high, even when the crowd is against you.

Lord, it's so hard when people turn on me. I hate that feeling! Help me through the seasons when I'm feeling picked on. I need Your courage and Your wisdom. Amen.

Hope Plays a Role

Be strong, be courageous, all you that hope in the LORD.
PSALM 31:24 GNT

Does hope play a role in being courageous? Sure! If you look at the mountain in front of you and suddenly feel hopeless, are you going to have the courage to speak to it? Probably not.

Let's look at that word *hope* for a minute. What does it mean to "hope in the Lord"?

When you hope something is going to happen, you look forward to it with a sense of expectation. Think about a little girl waiting for her birthday. She knows there's going to be a princess party, so she starts planning it well in advance. She knows which costume she's going to wear, which games the guests will play, and even which princess-worthy foods they will eat.

She's making plans for the party because she knows it's around the bend.

That's how hope is. It plans for the party, even when there's no hint of a party in sight. It says, "Hang in there—something better is coming!" even when circumstances don't look that way. Hope is the motivator that keeps you going, even when everyone around you says, "Girl, give it up."

Don't give up. Keep hoping. Keep believing. Keep trusting.

$$\gg\!\!\!\longrightarrow$$

I'll keep my hope in You, Jesus! You've never let me down and I know You never will. The party is coming! I can feel it! Amen.

The Real Truth

Don't be afraid of your enemies; always be courageous,
and this will prove to them that they will lose and that you
will win, because it is God who gives you the victory.
PHILIPPIANS 1:28 GNT

Have you ever thought about what it might be like to be a missionary? Missionaries really have to put themselves out there, don't they? Many have lost their lives sharing the gospel with hostile people who simply didn't want to hear it.

You don't have to be a full-time missionary to face opposition for your faith. It happens every day (way too often). People are hostile to the gospel message these days because it stands in opposition to many of the things they believe.

You know better, of course. You've read the Bible. (You have, right?) You know sin is sin, and you are doing your best to stand for what's right, even when it's hard.

Don't let your enemies (those who fight to be proven right) keep you from speaking truth, girl. Remember, it's not your truth you're speaking—it's God's truth. So be courageous. And here's some good news: He wins in the end! In other words, you will be proven right when you take a stand for truth, even if you don't see the victory today.

⟫⟫⟫———————→

I'll keep standing, Jesus! It's not easy. These enemies are like giant
mountains in my path sometimes. They say things that don't line up
with the Bible. But I know the real truth. It's found only in You. Amen.

A Watchman on the Wall

Be on your guard; stand firm in the faith; be courageous; be strong.
1 Corinthians 16:13 niv

Have you ever heard the phrase "be a watchman on the wall"? Back in Bible times, cities were surrounded by great walls. They served as protection from the enemies of the people who lived inside the city. But bad guys would come and try to climb the walls to attack the people inside. So "watchmen" were stationed on the walls. They had the job of making sure no one broke through the barrier.

God has placed you as a watchman on the wall. You were born at the right time and in the right place and to the right family, even if it doesn't always feel that way. You have work to do, and it's kingdom work!

Be on your guard. Stand firm in your faith. Be courageous and strong. In other words, be a watchman. Be diligent. Don't give up. Don't let the enemy of your soul break through the barricade. If you do, you won't be the only one hurt. He comes to steal, kill, and destroy, after all! So keep praying. Stay strong in your faith. And don't give way to the enemy, no matter what!

I get it, Jesus! The best way to knock down mountains is to not let them grow up in the first place! When I keep the enemy outside of the city walls, he can't wreak havoc. So with Your help I'll stay strong and courageous no matter what. Amen.

Hearts Melted in Fear

Now when all the Amorite kings west of the Jordan and all the Canaanite kings along the coast heard how the Lord had dried up the Jordan before the Israelites until they had crossed over, their hearts melted in fear and they no longer had the courage to face the Israelites.

JOSHUA 5:1 NIV

Consider this fascinating story from the book of Joshua. God's people, the Israelites, were hightailing it out of Egypt. They were headed across the desert to the Promised Land. Along the way they faced all sorts of obstacles. (Sound familiar? You're on your way to the Promised Land too, and you're facing obstacles!)

When the Israelites got to the Jordan River, God dried it up so that they could cross over. (He did the same thing at the Red Sea, when the enemy was chasing them down.) When word of what God had done got back to the bad guys (the Amorite and Canaanite kings), they panicked. They knew they probably shouldn't mess with God's people—not if He went to such great lengths to protect them!

You have enemies too. And they're watching closely. They see when God moves on your behalf. They're noticing when He comes through for you. And it causes them to be uncomfortable. Nervous. They know better than to mess with you when they see that God is on your side.

Don't ever be afraid. God can cause the hearts of those who oppose Him to quiver in fear!

Thank You for watching out for me, Jesus. You go before me and make my path smooth. My enemies are watching, and they know better than to mess with me! Amen.

Insecure Much?

I cling to you; your strong right hand holds me securely.
Psalm 63:8 nlt

Have you ever felt insecure? Let's unpack that word a little to see if we can get to the bottom of why we often feel that way.

When you feel secure, you feel safe. Add the prefix *in-* to the front of the word and it flips the meaning. You don't feel safe.

Picture a child in his father's arms. Dad releases his hold on the little one and tosses him up into the air. (Hey, we've probably all seen this done. It's unnerving, right?) There's no safety in being tossed in the air. For a couple of seconds, that little one's security flies right out the window.

Then Dad catches him.

That's kind of how life is. We go through situations where we feel like we lose all control. We're tossed into the air and imagine we'll land in a splat on the ground. Then our Father God catches us in His arms. Whew! Just in time too!

Things could have ended very badly, but He's right there, so close He can fix the problems right when they come up.

If you can trust Him to catch you when you fall, can't you also trust Him to move the mountains you're facing? Lay down your insecurities and watch as He takes care of you. . .every single time.

Thank You for catching me when I start to fall, Jesus!
I feel so insecure sometimes, so vulnerable. I'm so grateful
You're here for me when I'm feeling weak. Amen.

What a Gift!

With his own blood—not the blood of goats and calves—he entered the Most Holy Place once for all time and secured our redemption forever.
HEBREWS 9:12 NLT

Back in Old Testament times, God didn't forgive sin the way He does now. Jesus hadn't come yet, so the people couldn't just say, "God, please forgive me!" and expect it to happen.

Back then, the high priest would go into a special holy room called the Holy of Holies. He would "represent" the people. He was just one person, but he stood in the gap for all of them. He would sacrifice a spotless lamb and ask for God's forgiveness for the sins of all the people as the blood was shed.

When Jesus came, these sacrifices were no longer necessary. In a way, Jesus was like that spotless lamb. He never sinned. He was completely innocent. And yet He stood in the gap for you and for me. He died and rose again so that we could have eternal life. Jesus entered the Most Holy Place. What a gift He gave us! When you hear that, does it make you feel more secure in Him? You're His child, bought with a high price. There's no mountain high enough to undo what He did for you on the cross!

$\longrightarrow$

Thank You for that amazing gift, Jesus. You gave Your life so that I could have mine. I'm so grateful! Amen.

The Way He Sees You

You are altogether beautiful, my love; there is no flaw in you.
SONG OF SOLOMON 4:7 ESV

Do you see yourself the way God sees you? When you look in the mirror, do you say, "I'm beautiful!" or do you groan out loud?

Take a look at today's verse. The Lord thinks you are beautiful. When He looks at you through the blood of Jesus, as a redeemed child of God, He doesn't see any flaws. He sees only the perfection of Christ.

Does this truth change how you view yourself? It should! And think about this: one of the biggest mountains you'll face as a twenty-first-century teen girl is insecurity about your looks. (Hey, all girls go through it.) But you can speak to that mountain by simply repeating this verse to yourself.

You're beautiful, you know. Yes, you really are.

I want to see myself the way You do, Jesus! When I look in the mirror, I don't want to see my blemishes. I want to see past the physical and see a reflection of You—pure and righteous. Amen.

Wonderful Are Your Works!

I praise you, for I am fearfully and wonderfully made.
Wonderful are your works; my soul knows it very well.
PSALM 139:14 ESV

Imagine a toymaker in a shop, putting together a new toy. He works for hours—maybe even days or weeks—making sure it's absolutely perfect. Every square inch of the toy is carefully crafted and has a purpose.

That's how it was when God created you. He knit you together in your mother's womb. (That implies He took great time and care to create you.) In other words, He didn't just throw you together. His decisions were thoughtful. Deliberate. Without flaw.

Sure, you look at yourself and you see flaws. But knowing that you are fearfully and wonderfully made? That should change your perspective on those imperfections. A holy magnificence permeated your creation, a sense of awe and wonder as God meticulously formed your cells and wove your DNA.

Thank You for taking Your time with me, Jesus! I'm created in
Your image, in wonder and in awe. You don't make mistakes.
I know that in my heart. So I can trust that You made me
as I am—with a purpose and for a purpose. Amen.

Give Him Everything

*I appeal to you therefore, brothers, by the mercies of
God, to present your bodies as a living sacrifice, holy and
acceptable to God, which is your spiritual worship. Do not be
conformed to this world, but be transformed by the renewal
of your mind, that by testing you may discern what is the
will of God, what is good and acceptable and perfect.*
ROMANS 12:1–2 ESV

God calls you to present your body as a living sacrifice. That sounds painful, doesn't it?

Really, He's just saying that you need to use your body in a way that honors Him. And by "body" He's not just talking about your skin and bones. He's talking about your attitude. And your heart. And your mind.

He wants all of you, in other words. He created you to be like Him, and every time you live in a way that opposes Him, you're saying, "God, I don't really care how You created me. I'm going to do my own thing."

Don't do your own thing, girl. When you do, mountains rise up in front of you that were never meant to be there.

Live God's way and you'll discover love, joy, peace, and other great gifts straight from heaven. Offer every part of yourself to Him—heart, mind, body, soul, actions, thoughts. . .all of it. When you live that way, you bring honor to the one who created you in His image.

*I want to be like You in every way, Jesus! Today I offer
myself as a sacrifice, even if it hurts a little. I don't want
to do my own thing. I want to honor You. Amen.*

Be Sensible!

Sensible people accept good advice. People who talk
foolishly will come to ruin. Honest people are safe
and secure, but the dishonest will be caught.
PROVERBS 10:8–9 GNT

You want to do the right thing. You try to be sensible. But sometimes you find yourself saying and doing things that, well, shock you.

Take a look at today's verse. It says that people who talk foolishly will come to ruin. That doesn't sound very good, does it? On the other hand, honest people are safe and secure.

So how do you get past the point where you keep messing up? You won't. . .but you still keep trying. Do your best to be sensible. Sensible people make good decisions! When you live a foolish life, you invite trouble. You're pretty much saying to the mountains, "Hey, go right ahead! Rise up in front of me! Make my life difficult!"

And they will, you know. The further away from God you roam, the higher the mountains will grow.

Do your best to be honest and pure in His sight. Put away foolish talk. Try to be more like the one who made you. Then watch those mountains fade away at the mention of His name!

I want to bring honor to You, Jesus. I don't want to
dishonor You with the things I say. Help me to be
sensible and honest, not foolish and weak. Amen.

Look around You!

*"And you will feel secure, because there is hope;
you will look around and take your rest in security."*
JOB 11:18 ESV

How do you know you can trust God? Some people say you can't. They've given up on Him. There was a man in the Bible who almost reached that point, a guy named Job. Everything that could go wrong for a person went wrong for him. He lost his home, his children, his livestock. He lost his hope and almost lost his willingness to live.

No matter how low things get for you, you probably won't hit rock bottom the way Job did. But in the end, God restored everything he had lost. . .and then some!

Maybe that's why today's verse says, "Look around you!" God is in the restoration business! Sure, there are mountains. And yes, unfair things happen. There will be days you feel like you just can't keep going.

But. . .look around you! God is still on His throne. He provides food for you to eat and clothes for you to wear. You have a roof over your head and people who adore you.

Look around! He's given you life. . .the very breath in your lungs. And He has big things for you to do, girl, so don't you dare give up! Stay strong and secure in Him.

*I won't give up, Jesus! I'm looking around at all the
things You're still doing (even on my hard days),
and I have to admit. . .You're still in control! Amen.*

Snap Out of It!

"I will bring health and healing to [the city of Jerusalem]; I will heal my people and will let them enjoy abundant peace and security."
JEREMIAH 33:6 NIV

Sometimes you get down in the dumps. Admit it! When those days come, it's hard to snap out of it, even when everyone around you is saying you should.

Then you read a verse like this one from Jeremiah. And you're reminded that God's ultimate goal for you is to live in such health (spiritual, emotional, psychological, and physical) that you're able to do great things for Him. It's kind of hard to influence the world when you're down in the dumps, after all!

The enemy of your soul knows this, and he's happy to bring you down and try to keep you there. He knows you won't be effective for Jesus if you're always having a lousy day. But God, on the other hand, is wanting to snap you out of it, not just so you can accomplish big things, but because He adores you and wants the very best for you! Why else would He say that He's concerned about your health and prosperity?

Snap out of it, girl! You can walk securely in Him.

Thank You for reminding me that I can snap out of it, Jesus! I might be down in the dumps at times, but I don't have to stay there! I want to do great things for You! Amen.

He Will Pull You Out

*He pulled me out of a dangerous pit, out of the deadly
quicksand. He set me safely on a rock and made me secure.*
PSALM 40:2 GNT

If you've read the story of Joseph (in the Old Testament), you know that
his jealous brothers threw him into a pit to die. (They had some issues.) He
survived, but they ended up selling him into slavery. (And you thought *your*
siblings were trouble!)

Here's the thing: there will always be pits in life. You'll find yourself
trapped in them from time to time. Sometimes you're there because of
something you've done; other times you're there because someone else
shoved you down.

There is hope in the pit. That's the message of Joseph's story. Even when
you feel completely trapped, like all is lost. . .it isn't. God is with you in the
pit and He's there to help you climb out. He's not just a mountain-moving
God; He's a pit-climbing God!

No matter what you're facing today, no matter how deep the pit, cry out
to Jesus. Ask Him to help you out. He will, but you have to trust Him. Read
today's verse again and do your best to believe it. He's going to pull you out
and set you in a secure place. Trust Him.

*I will trust You to pull me from the deep, dark places, Jesus.
Thank You for setting me free and putting me in a safe place. Amen.*

Branded

And you also became God's people when you heard the
true message, the Good News that brought you salvation.
You believed in Christ, and God put his stamp of ownership
on you by giving you the Holy Spirit he had promised.
EPHESIANS 1:13 GNT

Have you ever seen cattle in a field? Most of the cows on large ranches are branded. The owner took a branding iron and put his mark on them. Why? So that if someone were to steal one of them, the owner could quickly identify it and bring it back home where it belongs.

God has put His mark on you. No, you're not physically branded. But He has put His seal (the Holy Spirit) inside of you. When the enemy tries to steal you away, God says, "Nope! Not this one! She's Mine, and I can prove it!"

Doesn't it bring you great comfort to know that the enemy will never steal you away from God? Oh, he'll try. He's pretty tricky. He'll place mountains in front of you and do his best to turn your trust away from the Lord. But he won't win. You're onto him.

Besides, you've been bought and paid for by the King of kings. You're His, girl. . .and no one else's!

I'm Yours, Jesus! You paid for me on the cross. And You put
Your stamp of ownership on me when You sent Your Spirit.
Nothing can steal my heart away—it's forever Yours! Amen.

Nothing Can Separate You

*And I am convinced that nothing can ever separate us from
God's love. Neither death nor life, neither angels nor demons,
neither our fears for today nor our worries about tomorrow—
not even the powers of hell can separate us from God's love. . .
Indeed, nothing in all creation will ever be able to separate us
from the love of God that is revealed in Christ Jesus our Lord.*
ROMANS 8:38–39 NLT

Nothing can separate you from God's love. You can mess up all day long
(ever been there?), and He won't stop loving you. You can turn your back on
Him (not recommended!), but He still won't give up on you. God adores you,
even on your worst possible day. And you have to admit, there have been
a few bad days in your life, days when you did things you weren't proud of.

His love for you isn't conditional. He doesn't say, "I'll only love you if. . ."
There are no ifs when it comes to His love for you. (Aren't you glad about that?)

You've no doubt found that your love for others is limited. You get irritated with people. You turn your back on some. You put your hand up and
say, "I don't want anything to do with you."

God, though? He'll never ever do that. You can rest secure in Him,
knowing He's going to go right on loving you, no matter how feisty you get.
Or how down in the dumps. Or how angry. Or how alienated. He's there for
you, ready to move mountains, even when you don't deserve it.

*I'll admit it, Jesus. . .I'm not always the most lovable person.
But You love me anyway and keep right on taking care
of me, even when I don't deserve it. I'm so grateful.*

The Mountain of Loneliness

He heals the brokenhearted and binds up their wounds.
PSALM 147:3 ESV

One of the mountains you may face in your life is the mountain of loneliness. It seems odd, doesn't it? You can be surrounded by people all day long and still feel lonely. Left out. Alone.

People aren't great at including others, especially girls. They push people to the outside of their circle. Oh, they don't always do it on purpose. Sometimes they're just so comfortable with their little cliques that they don't notice the ones who aren't included.

One way God will help you get rid of this mountain is to make you a friend to the friendless. So many others feel just like you do. They need—and want—a friend. They're feeling pushed out, excluded, and abandoned.

You can be a friend to the friendless. And in doing so, you may find that your own heart begins to heal. For in learning to love others, you'll discover that being a friend is a two-way street.

Be the initiator. Be the one who reaches out. Be the one who says, "Hey, is anyone sitting here?" when you see someone alone at the lunch table. Before long, you'll have friends in abundance, the ones God intended for you to reach.

*I want to learn how to be a good friend to others, Jesus.
I don't always know how to do that, but I know You can
help me! Thank You for showing me how to reach out, even
when doing so makes me a little nervous! Amen.*

He's Going to Meet Every Need

*And my God will supply every need of yours according
to his riches in glory in Christ Jesus.*

PHILIPPIANS 4:19 ESV

Has your family ever been through a rough financial season? When you're faced with a mortgage bill you can't pay or groceries you can't afford, it can feel like a mountain looming in front of you. It's so hard to know how to handle those situations when your bank account is sitting on empty.

God is still in the miracle-working business though. He owns the cattle on a thousand hills. And as the owner of it all, He has what you need even before you need it.

Think of that truth in light of today's verse. God promises to supply every need of yours—not from a bank account with limited funds, but according to His riches in glory in Christ Jesus. He has more than you could ever need already covered.

Trust Him. He'll move the financial mountains. He already has a plan to do so. He won't leave you or your family forsaken. Keep on asking. Keep on believing. Keep on trusting.

>>>———————→

*I know You're going to meet our needs, Jesus! You always
have and You always will. Until we see the miracle
happen, we'll keep trusting and believing! Amen.*

You're Part of the Family, Girl!

"For the LORD will not forsake his people, for his great name's sake, because it has pleased the LORD to make you a people for himself."
1 SAMUEL 12:22 ESV

Do you enjoy having "your people" together? Maybe you're at a family reunion, or the people you love have gathered together for Thanksgiving dinner. There's something kind of crazy and chaotic about your gatherings, but you wouldn't change them for anything.

Have you ever considered the fact that God loves to have His people too? Today's verse says it has pleased the Lord to make you a people for Himself. You're His, and He wants you to know it. And you know what it's like when you've got family around: they've got your back. No one can mess with you. That's how it is with God too. He has you totally covered. You're His kid, and no one's messing with you.

The enemy will try to cause problems, but think about what a family member would do if, say, a bad guy tried to break in the house. Your family member would take that guy down in a hurry, right? Same with God. He's not going to let the enemy win. So don't give up. You're part of a bigger family, one with a Dad who created the whole universe!

Thank You for sweeping me into the family, Lord. I'm so happy to belong! Amen.

Instructions from the Master

"Teach these new disciples to obey all the commands I have given you. And be sure of this: I am with you always, even to the end of the age."
MATTHEW 28:20 NLT

Right before Jesus ascended into heaven, He gave His disciples some parting instructions. Maybe you've been there. Your parents are going out for the evening and they're leaving you alone with your younger siblings. They're halfway out the door when they suddenly think of three or four more things you need to know. So they stop and quickly tell you, hoping you'll catch it all.

Jesus told His disciples two things: First, He instructed them to obey the commands He'd given them. The kind of commands He had given were different than the ones they had grown up hearing (from Old Testament days under the law). He taught them things like, "Do unto others as you would have others do unto you," and "Love your neighbor as yourself."

The second command He gave them was to be sure that He would always be with them. They needed this reminder, because He was about to disappear on them. But He had promised to send the Holy Spirit to live inside of them in His absence.

It's simple, really: remember to obey Jesus, and also remember that He won't leave you hanging. He's with you even now.

I won't forget, Jesus! I'll follow Your commands, loving people the way You love. And I'll remember that You're always with me! Amen.

Loud Sighing

O Lord, all my longing is before you; my sighing is not hidden from you.
Psalm 38:9 esv

You know what it feels like to sigh. Somehow, releasing that l-o-n-g, exaggerated breath makes you feel better, like you're breathing out the problem.

If you've ever been in a crowd and tried to stifle a sigh so that others wouldn't know you were upset, you know it's hard. Sometimes you pretend everything's okay when it's really not.

Take a look at today's verse. There's no point in trying to hide your sighing from God. He sees you every moment of your life. Every nanosecond. He knows when you're upset and when you're joyful, so there's no point in pretending with Him.

Maybe this is a day to get real with the Lord. Let Him hear your sighs loud and clear. Get those things you've been holding so tightly to off your chest. Tell Him your troubles. He sees those mountains, girl! He knows what you're dealing with. Share your heart. Let Him know how you feel about what you're up against. He can take it. And best of all, He will draw near to you as you draw near to Him. That's where the answers are found, after all—in His presence.

→→→→

*Here I am, Lord. I'm ready to tell You how I'm really feeling
about things. I know You can take it, so here goes. . . Amen.*

Your Gentle Heavenly Father

Turn to me, Lord, and be merciful to me, because I am lonely and weak.
PSALM 25:16 GNT

Have you ever had one of those days when you just prayed that everyone would treat you well, simply because you're so wiped out you can't think straight? (Sure, we've all been there!)

When you're really exhausted and weakened by life, it's hard to keep things in perspective when people aren't kind to you. You lash out. You lose it.

There's one who sees when you're having a hard day, and He's on the job, ready to treat you lovingly and gently. If you turn to God when you're having a rough day, He will respond by being merciful to you. He won't snap at you. He won't chew you out for not being at your best. Instead, He will see how lonely you are and how weak you feel. Instead of adding more mountains to your already stressful day, He'll gently wipe away your tears and give you the courage to keep going.

Some mountains are moved with gentleness. Aren't you glad you serve a gentle heavenly Father who sees and cares?

$\rightarrow\!\!\!\rightarrow\!\!\!\rightarrow$ ———————→

Thank You for Your mercy, Jesus! Your heart for me is filled with loving-kindness. I really need that, not just on the rough days, but every day. I'm so grateful for Your mercy. Amen.

The Mountain of Heartbreak

The LORD is near to the brokenhearted and saves the crushed in spirit.
PSALM 34:18 ESV

You've been through seasons when you felt absolutely crushed, like a giant sledgehammer had come down on you and smashed all the life out of you. Maybe you were wounded by a friend, someone you thought you could trust. Maybe you allowed yourself to like a boy, only to experience heartbreak or ridicule. Maybe your dad decided he didn't want to be married anymore and walked out on the family.

These things can really mess you up. When life hits you hard this way, it can be tempting to curl up in a ball and hide away from society. (Nap, anyone?) You lose faith in others and it's hard to know who you can trust.

Then God sweeps in, in His usual gentle way. He wipes away your tears and says, "Hey, I'm right here, and I'm not going anywhere. And by the way, you can totally trust Me, even with your broken heart."

He understands heartache, by the way. He experienced a lot of it on His way to the cross. So if anyone can be trusted with your broken heart, He can.

>>>———————→

I'm sorry You experienced heartache too, Jesus, but I'm so glad You understand what I'm going through. Thank You for always being there for me. I love You and trust You, even when the mountain of heartbreak rises up! Amen.

Come Home with Me!

"I will not leave you as orphans; I will come to you."
JOHN 14:18 ESV

Have you ever visited an orphanage? Maybe you went on a mission trip and stopped at an orphanage. Playing with the kids was fun, but then you had to leave and go back home to your comfortable house with that cute bedroom and lots of food in the pantry and refrigerator.

Only, the kids you visited didn't get to go home. Those children had to stay in the orphanage with no parents to love them. And you felt sick inside, thinking about it. Would they ever be adopted? Would anyone ever say, "Hey, you're mine! Come home with me!"?

Now look at today's verse. Jesus promises that He won't leave us as orphans. We'll never have to experience the heartache of feeling unwanted or unloved. We'll never be truly alone. He has promised to come to us when we're feeling abandoned. He sweeps in and comforts us, saying, "Hey, girl! Lift that head! You're My child, and and I adore you!"

He does, you know.

---

*Thank You for adopting us, Father God! I'm so glad
to be Your daughter. I'm safe and secure with You,
never abandoned and never truly alone. Amen.*

Never Alone

Then the LORD God said, "It is not good that the man should be alone; I will make him a helper fit for him."
GENESIS 2:18 ESV

God never meant for people to live life completely alone. He always wanted us to have companionship and a tight circle to experience life with.

Think about Adam, alone in the garden. He spent a lot of time with God, talking to Him, sharing his heart. Even so, God still thought Adam needed another human in the picture. That's why He created Eve to fill that missing space in Adam's life.

You need people too. The enemy will try to raise up relationship problems to convince you that you don't need—or want—people in your life. He'll try to convince you that you're better off on your own. But girl, God never meant for you to live like that. You need the love, advice, and joy that others can bring—friends, family, neighbors, and your community. Yes, even that pesky boy at school who drives you crazy. God has filled your world with people. . .on purpose.

Don't try to do life alone. When relational mountains rise, speak to them in Jesus' name and watch them fall so that you can experience life in community.

*I get it, Jesus. I shouldn't pull away from people,
even when they hurt me. I see how the enemy is trying
to get me alone, and I won't let his tactics work! I'll open
myself back up to loving people. Help me, I pray. Amen.*

Get Alone to Pray

But He would withdraw to desolate places and pray.
LUKE 5:16 ESV

It's true that God wants us to live in community, and it's also true that He's always surrounding us with people we can learn from. But if we look at the life of Jesus, we see that He sometimes pulled away. . .on purpose. He would go to "desolate places" to pray.

So what is a desolate place? Do you have to travel to the desert or some faraway island to be alone with Him?

The word *desolate* means "a place empty of people." So. . .no, you don't have to travel to a faraway place to spend time with God. You simply have to step away from the crowd for a while to pray and to reconnect with your Savior.

Where is your desolate place? Your bedroom, maybe? A park in your neighborhood? Your backyard? Your closet?

You can turn any area into a prayer room if you think about it. And you can step away from the chaos, the madness, the chatter to a quiet, desolate place with Him.

———⟩⟩⟩————————→

*Thanks for this reminder to break away from the craziness
to hang out with You, Jesus. I won't let too much time
go by! I'll never face the mountain of loneliness as long
as I remember to hide away with You. Amen.*

Molehills

*They do not fear bad news; they confidently
trust the LORD to care for them.*
PSALM 112:7 NLT

Have you ever known someone who always seemed to be expecting the worst? Maybe she had a pain in her side and immediately suspected appendicitis. Or maybe she got a bad grade on a test and flipped out, convinced she would never make it into the college of her choice.

There's a funny little saying, "Don't make mountains out of molehills." A molehill is a tiny thing, but some people make h-u-g-e deals out of small ones. They blow each little obstacle into Mount Everest.

Don't be like that. You'll spend your whole life overwhelmed if you panic at every little thing. See the molehills as what they are: tiny. Easily overcome.

And remember, even the mountains will fall when you speak to them in faith. So even if the tiny thing turns out to be a big thing, you can rest assured that God will still help you through it.

→→→————————→

*I'll admit it, Lord—sometimes I overreact! I see a tiny little
molehill and it looks like a giant mountain to me. So I freak
out! I panic. I get overwhelmed and think all hope is lost.
Help me to see things in perspective. Give me Your eyes
to see those "little things" for what they are. Amen.*

Some Trust in Chariots

Some trust in chariots and some in horses, but we
trust in the name of the LORD our God.
PSALM 20:7 ESV

What does it mean to trust in chariots and horses? What an interesting phrase!

Back in the olden days, the kings and warriors often went to battle. Things were a little different back then. They didn't do war the way it's fought now, with missiles and planes. In those days, it all came down to the horses and chariots (basically war machines).

When the battle was hot and heavy, a good horse and chariot were critical. Otherwise you wouldn't win. So perhaps the writer of this psalm is really saying, "When the going gets tough, you shouldn't put your trust in the vehicle. Put your trust in God."

It's so easy to put our trust in the obvious things—money, good grades, great friends, and so on. Some of those things might be helpful during a battle, but ultimately, trusting in God is the only thing that will save us.

———————————→

I will trust in You alone, Jesus! I know there will be obstacles. There will
be battles. But the only way I'll make it through is with You at my side.
So I put my total trust in You—not just today, but every day! Amen.

Mere Mortals

When I am afraid, I put my trust in you. In God,
whose word I praise—in God I trust and am not
afraid. What can mere mortals do to me?
PSALM 56:3–4 NIV

"What can mere mortals do to me?"

Sounds like something a superhero would say, right? "You mere mortals cannot touch me! I am untouchable!"

And yet that's exactly what you are as a daughter of the King. Satan will do his best to trip you up, but in the end, you're a princess who's incapable of being taken down. Why? Because Jesus is on your side. That makes you untouchable!

So. . .yes, mortals will try to mess with you. The kids at school. Your siblings. Your cousins. That annoying boy down the street. Even some of the adults in your world will bug you. But ultimately, mortals don't have a say in how your story ends. That's up to God and God alone. (Hint: He not only knows the end of the story but also has a plan for a true happily-ever-after!)

You'll face mountains. Some of them will look like people. Just remember, they're mortals. They have no real power like the power of your Savior!

$\longrightarrow$

I'll put my trust in You, Lord, not in people! Jesus, You're the most
powerful of the powerful! I'm so glad You're on my side! Amen.

Perfect Peace

*You will keep in perfect peace those whose minds are
steadfast, because they trust in you. Trust in the LORD forever,
for the LORD, the LORD himself, is the Rock eternal.*
ISAIAH 26:3–4 NIV

Have you ever stepped away from the swirling craziness of life and just gone for a quiet walk? Maybe you live in a neighborhood with a little lake or pond. Or maybe you live in the country, where the roads are still and quiet in the evenings.

It's so great to clear your mind of the clutter. In that peaceful place you can draw closer to God. You can hear His voice with more clarity. You can worship with a freedom you don't often experience when you're surrounded by people, places, and things.

Take a look at today's verse. God promises to keep you in perfect peace when your mind is steadfast, when you place your trust in Him. Sometimes it takes literally stepping away from the madness to get there.

Feeling stuck? Go for a walk. Feeling upset, frustrated, or worked up? Step away. Go into a different room. Hide in the bathroom. Go in the backyard. Go for a swim. When you separate yourself from the chaos, you will finally have a chance to do the one thing that will make a difference—spend time with the one who is capable of moving mountains.

*I get so worked up sometimes, Jesus! But I'm surrounded by noise.
My life is so busy, so hectic. Thank You for the reminder that my
mind can be at peace if I keep my thoughts on You. Show me how
to do that, even in the middle of the craziness, I pray. Amen.*

If. . .Then!

Commit your way to the LORD; trust in him, and he will act.
PSALM 37:5 ESV

Here's an "if" verse for you! "If" you commit your way to the Lord, "if" you trust in Him, "then" He will act.

Maybe you're wondering if God falls asleep at the wheel when you're going through tough seasons. Doesn't He see you? Doesn't He care? Why doesn't He sweep in and fix everything right away?

Then you read a verse like this one and you realize you have a role to play too. You've got to do your part, girl!

So here are some tough questions: Have you committed your journey to the Lord? Totally, fully, completely? Have you said, "Jesus, please have Your way in my life, even if Your way doesn't match up with my way"? Have you trusted Him, even when the situations swirling around you are hard to understand?

If you do those two things, you can count on God taking action. If He's moving too slowly for you, then ask yourself, *Is He waiting on me to do my part, maybe?*

Could be, He is!

Lord, I won't keep You waiting. Today I choose to recommit my life to You. Even if Your plan for my life looks different from mine, I'll totally trust You. Thank You for knocking down the mountains in front of me! Amen.

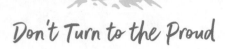

Don't Turn to the Proud

*Blessed is the man who makes the LORD his trust, who does
not turn to the proud, to those who go astray after a lie!*
PSALM 40:4 ESV

Imagine you were asked to go on a hike with two friends. The three of you
came to a fork in the road and one of your friends—the prideful one—insisted
you all turn to the right. The other friend, much humbler, quietly said, "I really
feel like the road to the left is the one we should take."

Your prideful friend took off in a huff, not even caring if you followed.
Your quiet friend shrugged and looked your way.

What would you do?

This seems like a funny illustration, maybe, but that's kind of how life
is sometimes. When you chase after the wrong people, places, and things,
you end up lost.

Don't go astray. If you do, you'll accidentally create more mountains
than you expected in your life. Follow hard after God, and when you come
to a fork in the road, listen to His still, small voice. He'll show you which
way to go, and it will be the route that leads to life, peace, and joy.

➤➤➤————————→

*I get it, Jesus. I've been at a fork in the road lots of times!
Some of my friends push me in the wrong direction.
I'll confess, I've followed after them at times! But no more!
From now on, I want to always follow hard after You! Amen.*

Take Refuge in Him

It is better to take refuge in the LORD than to trust in man.
PSALM 118:8 ESV

The Bible has a lot of interesting words in it! Take the word *refuge*, for instance. Back in Bible times, a refuge was a safe place to hide away. When your enemies were hot on your tail, you could hide in the cleft of a rock or maybe in a cave. These refuges offered the one being chased a minute to catch his breath and figure out what to do next.

You might not have a literal enemy on your tail, but the enemy of your soul is continually trying to trip you up. You go to friends for advice, which is good, but there is one who has even better advice than all your wisest friends put together. God is waiting, hiding away in the cleft of the rock, ready to give you the answers you need. But you have to go there. Spend time with Him. Take refuge in Him long enough to catch your breath. Let Him show you the next step and help you to strategize so that you can be set free once and for all.

I'll take refuge in You, Jesus. . .not in people! They might have great advice (some of them), but Yours is the best. You're the only one I can truly trust. So lay it on me! I'm ready to hear what You have to say! Amen.

Take Time Off

"Come to me, all who labor and are heavy laden, and I will give you rest. Take my yoke upon you, and learn from me, for I am gentle and lowly in heart, and you will find rest for your souls. For my yoke is easy, and my burden is light."
MATTHEW 11:28–30 ESV

Have you ever been so exhausted, so run down, that nothing made sense anymore? Maybe you got in over your head with activities and fell behind on your schoolwork. Or maybe you struggled in a particular relationship and couldn't sleep at night because you were so worked up about it.

These things happen.

There's a reason God took a day off on the Sabbath. He was leading by example, to show us how important it is for our bodies, hearts, minds, and spirits to get some much-needed rest.

When you're not rested, you make wrong decisions. You get confused. You get cranky. And when you're wiped out, you're more inclined to see tiny obstacles as huge ones.

Get some rest, girl. Kick your feet up. Take a bubble bath. Climb under the covers an hour earlier than usual. Take some time to get refreshed so that you're more alert during the daytime and better able to battle those mountains that rise up.

Catch some z's. You'll be glad you did!

I'm so tired tonight, Jesus. Helpl me to relax and refresh, so I'll be good as new for tomorrow.

Breakthrough Is Coming!

So let's not get tired of doing what is good. At just the right time we will reap a harvest of blessing if we don't give up.
GALATIANS 6:9 NLT

Picture a farmer out in his field. It's almost harvest season, but he's feeling down in the dumps. Things aren't moving fast enough to please him. So he walks away just before the crop is ready to be harvested. He gives up, just on the brink of his miracle. Sad, right? If only he believed what he could not yet see!

That's how it is with you sometimes too. You get tired of waiting on God. You think things like, *I just can't do this faith thing anymore.* And you give up. You walk away, convinced that God has failed you and that He can't be trusted.

Oh, but He *can* be trusted! And you'll never know how close you are to seeing those mountains fall if you walk away, girl! So stick around, even during the hard seasons. Remember that old saying: It's always darkest just before the dawn. Dawn is coming. Breakthrough is on its way. But you have to stick around or you'll miss it. What a tragedy that would be!

$$\longrightarrow$$

Okay, okay! I'll stick around, Jesus. I won't give up when things don't seem to be going my way. I'll keep trusting. I'll keep believing. And I'll (eventually) see those mountains fall! Amen.

Reaching Out to the Hurting

I have the highest confidence in you, and I take great
pride in you. You have greatly encouraged me and
made me happy despite all our troubles.
2 CORINTHIANS 7:4 NLT

Have you ever considered the fact that you might be usable to God? Maybe He wants to use you today to lift up someone who's going through depression. It's possible that your words—kind, thoughtful, and positive—could be enough to turn someone's attitude (and eventually their situation) around. Did you realize your words have that kind of power? They do!

Think about the story behind today's verse. After Jesus ascended into heaven, the disciples were left to do the work of spreading the gospel. Sometimes this work could be really depressing. Many of them were imprisoned for their faith or faced great opposition as they spread the word. (And you thought your life was hard!)

But look at this verse, written by Paul to his new converts: "You have greatly encouraged me and made me happy despite all our troubles." A few kind words from his friends was all he needed to turn his bad day around.

When you see a friend who's struggling today, say something kind. She has mountains in her life, and you can help move them with just a word!

I'll do my best to speak positive words over my friends,
Jesus! Help me to be uplifting. I want to touch those
who are hurting and bring hope. Amen.

Near to the Brokenhearted

When the righteous cry for help, the Lord hears and delivers them out of all their troubles. The Lord is near to the brokenhearted and saves the crushed in spirit.
PSALM 34:17–18 ESV

Imagine a little girl sleeping in her bed at night. She wakes up to a strange noise and it scares her, so she cries out. But her parents don't hear her. So she stays in her bed, petrified, frozen in place, unwilling to go to them for fear the boogeyman will get her.

Maybe you've been there. You went through a dark season and felt like no one saw your pain or depression. You did your best to cry out, but no one seemed to notice. So you sat frozen, locked in place.

Sweet girl, God is near to the brokenhearted. You might not "feel" like it, but He is. He's closer than your next cry. He's ready, willing, and able to step in. From your perspective, He might seem a hundred light-years away. But He heard you. He hears you even now. Today's verse promises that He will save those who are crushed in spirit. Trust Him, no matter how low you feel.

Lord, I trust You! I'm so grateful that You hear me and that You care. You more than care! You jump into action and take care of the things I'm struggling with. I'm so grateful You're always there for me, ready to move mountains, even before I cry out!

Walk Free, Girl!

*But you, LORD, are a shield around me, my glory,
the One who lifts my head high.*
PSALM 3:3 NIV

You've been low. Deep in the valley. And when you're down there, the shadows are all you see. Sunlight is invisible to you. So you hunker down and learn to adapt to your darkened environment. Up above you hear signs of life from other people. You wish you could join them, but it just seems impossible. You're stuck, and no one can help you up.

Only, there is one who can! Depression is a serious condition, especially if it blossoms and grows. But God can move the mountain of depression, no matter how deep the valley you're in. Reach out to Him, of course, but also have the courage to reach out to someone else in your life you trust.

Today is your day. Don't let the depression go on any longer. Pick up the phone and let someone know. Tell a teacher. Or a counselor. Or a trusted friend or neighbor or parent.

You can be set free from depression. You can watch that mountain move in Jesus' name. It might take the help of a counselor, doctor, or friend, but with God on your side, you don't have to remain in the valley any longer.

Walk free, girl!

*I'm ready to come out of the valley, Jesus! I see glimpses of sunlight
up above, and I want to join those who are living life to the fullest.
Show me who to reach out to. I want to walk free! Amen.*

Believe Also in Jesus

"Let not your hearts be troubled. Believe in God; believe also in me."
JOHN 14:1 ESV

Jesus told His followers to believe not just in His Father (God) but also in Him. Why do you suppose He said that?

Many people who met Jesus simply didn't believe He was the Son of God. It was a pretty radical claim, after all. (If you met a guy who said that, what would you think?)

Of course, He backed up that claim by performing miracle after miracle. His supernatural abilities were undeniable! And He knew that if He could convince His followers to believe that He was the Christ, the Son of the living God, they would automatically let go of their fears and anxieties.

When you're holding on to worries and fears, are you truly believing in Him, or have you given up? (It's a tough question, but maybe it's time to be honest.) Often we just give up. We see the circumstances and think, *This isn't going to end well.*

With Jesus in the picture, the story *will* end well. You can have a true happily-ever-after. So invite Him in, girl! Believe also in Jesus!

→

*I believe in You, Jesus. You really are the Savior. You really
can set me free! You really are working miracles, even now!
I'm so glad You're the King of my heart! Amen.*

Let It Go!

Leave all your worries with him, because he cares for you.
1 PETER 5:7 GNT

Have you ever accidentally left something behind? Maybe you leave the mall and don't realize you've somehow dropped your phone. Or your wallet. Or your purse.

Or maybe you come home from school and you're getting ready to study for a test, only you realize you left the book at school by accident. These things happen.

Leaving something behind is a weird feeling, isn't it?

Now think about that in light of today's verse. God wants you to deliberately leave behind your worries. Drop them off and forget about them. Don't go back and search for them, like you would your purse. Don't try to pick them back up again once you've let them go. Once they're out of your hands, do your best to move forward without them.

Why does God want you to let go of your worries? Because He cares for you. He knows that hanging on to your worries means hanging on to the pain. And He loves you way too much to see you do that, girl. So let it go.

I get so tired of hanging on to stuff that I should let go of, Jesus. But sometimes it's hard to release my grip and drop the things that are bugging me. (Hanging on is easier sometimes.) I need Your help to let go! Please move this mountain of worry so that I can let it go once and for all! Amen.

Fake It Till You Make It? No Way!

When people are happy, they smile, but when
they are sad, they look depressed.
PROVERBS 15:13 GNT

Have you ever heard the phrase "Fake it till you make it"? Some people are really good at it. You would never know they're going through something awful because they have bright smiles plastered on their faces!

You, though? You're not always so good at faking it. . .and that's okay. God actually prefers honesty, even if it's gut honesty.

Don't try to hide your sadness if you're going through a rough patch. Don't hide away from others and plaster a smile on your face, pretending everything's okay when it's really not.

God wants you to be real—with Him and with others. It's not going to be easy, and it will mean you'll have to be vulnerable. But what good will it do you to go on lying, saying everything's fine?

Be real. You'll be so glad you let go of the pretending.

I'm sorry for trying to force a smile when I was really hurting
inside, Jesus. I know You've always wanted to heal me.
Please touch my heart today, once and for all. Amen.

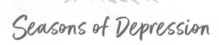

Seasons of Depression

*I was depressed and ill for several days. Then I got up and
went back to the work that the king had assigned to me,
but I was puzzled by the vision and could not understand it.*
DANIEL 8:27 GNT

Have you ever walked through a season of depression? Maybe you felt like you were in a slump and couldn't seem to snap out of it. It's hard, once you're down, to get back up again.

If you read the Old Testament, you'll find story after story of people who faced depression. Daniel. Moses. David. Elijah. Hannah. So many of the people of God walked through valleys. And guess what? Every single one of them rose from the ashes to do great things for God.

You'll rise too. You just need to stay focused on Him and not your problems. Don't let the valley grab hold of you and convince you that you'll never come back out into the sunlight again. You can. . .and you will. Sure, there are times when the depression is severe enough that you need medical intervention. But even then, the Lord can point you in the right direction.

Your mountain of depression isn't bigger than God. Read that again. The mountain of depression that you're facing is no match for the Creator of heaven and earth. He can handle your valley. In fact, He's building a road out of it even now.

―――――――――▶

*I trust You in the valley, Lord! You can reach down low to
the depths, where I find myself sometimes. I'm walking out
of this low place into the sunlight, with Your help. Thank
You for setting me free from depression. Amen.*

What's the Point?

This is the case of a man who is all alone, without a child or a brother, yet who works hard to gain as much wealth as he can. But then he asks himself, "Who am I working for? Why am I giving up so much pleasure now?" It is all so meaningless and depressing.
ECCLESIASTES 4:8 NLT

What's the point of all this? Maybe you've asked yourself that question at times. Sometimes we work, work, work. . .and for what?

Example: You join this club and that club. You attend this event and that event. You go, go, go. . .until you're so worn out you can barely function. Then you wonder why you're facing so many obstacles. Many are there because you've overloaded yourself!

Staying excessively busy is a good habit to break when you're a teen so that you're not overloaded as an adult. Things can get complicated when you're older because a paycheck will probably be involved. (Hey, it's easy to go chasing after more money, right?) Only, God wants you to chase after Him, not money. Not stuff.

Today's pleasures are tomorrow's headache. No, it's true. The things that seem fun and exciting today all too often become your worst enemy tomorrow. So stop chasing after bigger and better. If you're going to chase anything, let it be Him.

———————⟫———————→

You're the only thing that satisfies, Lord! I don't want to crave anything but You! I've tried the pleasures of this world, and they've led to depression and pain. May I find my true joy in You alone! Amen.

Low Places

Come quickly, LORD, and answer me, for my depression
deepens. Don't turn away from me, or I will die.
PSALM 143:7 NLT

The writer of this psalm was in a l-o-w place. Super low. So low that he needed (and wanted) intervention. . .immediately.

Have you ever been there? Have you ever cried out to God, saying something like this: "Lord, if You don't send someone to reach out to me immediately, I don't know if I'm going to make it through this!"?

That's a low place. But read the rest of the verse. (Here's where you find God's answer!) "Don't turn away from Me."

Let's unpack that for a moment. In order for someone to turn away, that would have to mean they're watching you closely. Their eyes are on you. They see. They understand.

God is watching. He's as close as your next breath. He sees your salty tears. And He not only sees; He cares. He feels the depth of your pain and He's not—repeat, *not*—turning away. He'll never turn His back on you.

He adores you. He's there for you. He's not going to let you down. So rise up, girl!

I've been in a low place, Lord. This depression has convinced me
I'm stuck. Thank You for not turning Your back on me. It brings
me such hope to know this mountain won't loom in front of me
forever. You've got the answer, Jesus! You are the answer. Amen.

A Broken Heart

"My heart is broken. Depression haunts my days."
JOB 30:16 TLB

What does it mean to have a broken heart? Is it possible for a heart to be physically broken?

Maybe you've experienced the pain of heartbreak. Someone you loved turned against you. A boy you cared for hurt you terribly. Or maybe your parents divorced and one of them abandoned the family.

These sorts of betrayals and life changes can be deeply hurtful. And it's easy during those seasons to want to give up on others, to say, "I'll never love again. People are no good."

Sweet girl, don't let the pain of heartbreak lock you in its prison. That's no way to live! Yes, you'll be hurt from time to time. Sure, you'll be depressed and lonely. These things happen. But God has a bright future for you, and you're going to miss it if you pull away from the people He's placed in your world.

Heartbreak isn't permanent. And God has holy superglue to piece that broken heart back together again, no matter how deep the pain is at this very moment.

Trust Him. That heart will heal. You have His word on it.

>>>———————→

*I will take You at Your word, Jesus! You want to heal
me from depression. Point me toward a bright future,
Lord! I'll get there with Your hand in mine! Amen.*

Peer Pressure: A Looming Mountain

Don't do as the wicked do, and don't follow the path
of evildoers. Don't even think about it; don't go
that way. Turn away and keep moving.
PROVERBS 4:14–15 NLT

Imagine you're standing in a small room and the walls start to close in around you. Closer and closer they come, until you can reach out and touch them. The pressure of those walls begins to scare you. Will they crush you?

That might seem like an extreme example, but that's kind of how peer pressure affects you. It's a wall closing in on you. It's a mountain looming large in front of you.

The only way to escape the mountain of peer pressure is to step away from it completely. You can't allow it in your life. You know what you need to do. You have friends who put that kind of pressure on you. They won't be happy until your room is so small that you have no choice but to do what they tell you.

Only, God wants you to live in freedom. He can speak a word and those walls can tumble to the ground, just like the walls of Jericho fell for Joshua in the Old Testament.

Don't allow the walls to close. Don't allow so-called friends to mold you into their image. Be set free, girl. Step away from tiny spaces and live large!

$$\rightarrow\rightarrow\rightarrow\longrightarrow$$

I'm done with living in compressed spaces, Lord! I'm tired of people
telling me how to live. I simply need to be like You. Please show me
how to break free from the mountain of peer pressure. Amen.

Don't Make Friends with Them

Keep company with the wise and you will become wise.
If you make friends with stupid people, you will be ruined.
PROVERBS 13:20 GNT

Can we just pause to look at the words *stupid people* a moment? Do you not find it entertaining that God would tell you not to make friends with stupid people? Funny, right?

Stupid people do stupid things. And they try to make *you* do stupid things. Don't link arms with stupid people. You'll be sorry, because they will rub off on you whether you want them to or not. And if this verse is correct (hint: it is!), they will lead you to ruin. In other words, they will take you as far down the trail of stupid as you let them, until you totally crash and burn.

That's not God's plan for you. He offers a better way, and it starts with hanging out with the wise ones, the ones making good decisions. Today's verse says, "Keep company with the wise and you will become wise." Hey, we do become like those we hang out with. Just one more reason not to keep company with fools. You can see how that will end, right?

→

I get it, Jesus! There are plenty of foolish people in my
world, but I don't have to become best friends with them.
Show me how to keep my distance and still be a light
to them. I want to be wise, not foolish. Amen.

Skip the People Pleasing, Please!

For am I now seeking the approval of man, or of God?
Or am I trying to please man? If I were still trying to
please man, I would not be a servant of Christ.
GALATIANS 1:10 ESV

Whose approval are you seeking? Maybe you want your friends to notice you and be impressed by what you do. Or how you dress. Or how smart you are. Or how talented. Or how pretty. Nothing is necessarily wrong with wanting to be noticed, for the most part.

But if you're looking for others' approval above God's, you're going to wind up in the people-pleasing business—and that always creates more problems than solutions. Pleasing people can be exhausting, after all. And let's face it—no matter how hard you try, most people aren't going to give you pats on the back for every little thing. Many of them won't even notice the lengths to which you're going to get noticed, honestly.

God will give you all the pats you need. He thinks you're pretty amazing, after all. So don't let the mountain of "people pleasing" rise up in front of you for long. Instead, rest easy in the love and admiration the Creator of heaven and earth has for you. His opinion means so much more than anyone else's!

Show me how to get over being a people pleaser, Jesus! I don't want this
to be a thing in my life. I care about what You think. . .above all. Amen.

Bad Company

Do not be fooled. "Bad companions ruin good character."
Come back to your right senses and stop your sinful ways.
I declare to your shame that some of you do not know God.
1 CORINTHIANS 15:33–34 GNT

We face a lot of mountains in our lives that don't have to be there. Sometimes those obstacles come as a direct result of the friendships we are keeping. (Ever been there?)

Maybe you have a friend whose behaviors are the opposite of yours. She has no limits, no godly boundaries. She does all sorts of things you would never consider doing, and she flaunts her lifestyle in front of you, even making fun of you for not joining in.

If you let this girl have too much power over you, she can become a negative influence in your life. Before long, you'll find that your boundaries are slipping too. Your language. Your behavior. Your attitude. Your actions.

Bad company ruins good character. The enemy of your soul isn't just after your attitude; he wants to win you over, totally and completely. He wants you to give up on godly living and enter into a lifestyle that pleases him instead. And he's sly, that tricky devil! He has strategically placed "friends" in your path to ease you in his direction.

Come back to your right senses. You have to wake up from your spiritual slumber and see the truth of what Satan is doing. Do not be fooled. Eyes wide open, girl. The enemy is on the prowl, but you're smarter than he is!

→

I won't be fooled, Jesus. My eyes are open to what Satan
is doing. I won't turn away from godly living, even if those
around me do. I'll stick with Your plan, Lord. Amen.

One Bad Apple

The righteous choose their friends carefully,
but the way of the wicked leads them astray.
PROVERBS 12:26 NIV

Imagine you're standing inside the grocery store's produce department, looking at a barrel of apples. You pick up three of them and start to put them into a clear bag to add to your cart. Only, just as you put them in the bag, you realize one of them has a bad spot on it. So you put it back.

Why? Because, as the old saying goes, "one bad apple can spoil the whole bunch." It's true! If you purchased all three apples, the "diseased" one would eventually cause the others to rot. You would lose all of them, simply because of the one.

Now consider this information in light of your friendships. One bad apple can spoil the whole bunch. This is why the righteous choose their friends carefully, because there are always people out there ready to pull you in the wrong direction.

Choose wisely. Not everyone is meant to be in your friend group, girl. It might be time to step away from the ones who are constantly tugging you to do the wrong thing. They're building mountains instead of tearing them down.

This is a hard one, Lord! I have friends I care about
who always seem to be doing the wrong thing. . .
on purpose. Show me how to back away! Amen.

At All Times

A friend loves at all times, and a brother is born for a time of adversity.
PROVERBS 17:17 NIV

A friend loves at all times. Read those words again. Let's be honest: not every friend is easy to love all the time. You have a few (you know who they are) who wear you out. There have been times you've said to yourself, *This one's not worth it. She's too much work!*

Aren't you glad God doesn't look at you that way? You are a lot of work to Him, whether you want to admit it or not. You're not always the best friend to Him that you should be, but He's not planning to give up on you. . .ever.

Now take another look at today's verse. A brother is born for adversity. A "brother" is a friend of the very closest sort. This is the one you know you can always go to, even in the middle of a crisis. Or when you've fallen so far from God that you don't think anyone else will accept you. He's that "brother" you can trust with your life.

That's the kind of friend God is to you, always. He's closer than a brother. And He'll show you how to be that sort of friend to others.

⟫⟶

Thank You for the friends who haven't abandoned me, Jesus. Show me how to be more like You so that I can be that kind of friend too. Amen.

Following after God

Come, my young friends, and listen to me,
and I will teach you to honor the Lord.
PSALM 34:11 GNT

Do you think that following after God comes naturally? Ask the disciples! They gave up everything to follow after Jesus, and things weren't always easy for them. In fact, many of them faced persecution and pain.

No one said that following after Jesus would be easy. It's a process, but it's one that will ultimately work to your advantage. Only in following after Him will you truly become all you were meant to be. Only in chasing hard after Him will you be able to speak to mountains. Only in loving and worshipping Him will you find total fulfillment in life.

Imagine the Lord calling out to you with His arms outstretched. He's inviting you into His inner circle, longing to spend quality time with you.

You can hear from Him by reading His Word (the Bible) but also by spending time in prayer. Jesus considers you a student. You're on a learning curve. You won't get it all right, but be the best pupil you can. Why? So that you can please His heart, sure, but also so that you can live your very best life!

You call. . .and I respond, Jesus! I will come and spend time with
You as a happy student, ready to honor You with my life. Amen.

Don't Give In!

My child, when sinners tempt you, don't give in.
PROVERBS 1:10 GNT

You will be tempted. Probably multiple times a day, in fact. Even Jesus faced temptation. The enemy tempted Him when He went to the wilderness to fast and pray.

But just because you're tempted doesn't mean you have to give in. Just because a mountain rises up in front of you doesn't mean you have to go skiing on it.

You can avoid temptation. You can walk around that mountain. You can speak to that mountain and watch it fall. You can tell that mountain it has no place in your life.

No matter how you're being tempted today—to cheat, to lie, to smoke, to drink, to hang out with the wrong crowd—you have the power inside of you to say no.

Jesus said no when the devil tempted Him. (Think of how different the gospel story would be if He had given in!) He was showing you that you don't have to give in. Yes, it will be hard at times. No, you don't have to fall for the enemy's tricks.

You can say no. Please say no.

———⟩⟩⟩————→

*I'll say no today, Jesus. No to the wrong things. No to temptation.
No to the wrong crowd. No to things that are dangerous or
things that aren't Your best for me. Thank You for the reminder
that I have the ability to say no and walk away. Amen.*

Who to Hang Out With

I am a friend to all who fear you, to all who follow your precepts.
PSALM 119:63 NIV

Wondering who you should hang out with? Want to know who you can trust in this world? Become a friend to those who are friends with Jesus. It's really that simple. You know a fake from the real deal. You know when someone is just pretending to have a relationship with God to pull one over on their parents or church leaders.

God wants you to have real, genuine relationships with people who run deep with Him. These are the people you can turn to when you face mountains. They will stand shoulder to shoulder with you and help you speak to those mountains so that you can watch them fall.

If you were forming a football team, wouldn't you want the best players on your team? Choosing to hang out with other Christ followers is kind of the same thing. You're here on this planet to do great things for God. How awesome to be surrounded by like-minded people who have the same goals. Together, you will accomplish so much for the kingdom of God.

Hang with the right people, girl.

I'm so excited when I think about all the people You've placed in my life, Jesus! You are showing me how to do great things for You, and You're even giving me the right people for my team! I'm so grateful. Amen.

A Good Strategy

Do not go where evil people go. Do not follow the example of the
wicked. Don't do it! Keep away from evil! Refuse it and go on your way.
PROVERBS 4:14–15 GNT

Don't go where evil people go. Really, if we could just grab ahold of that strategy and stick with it, we would avoid a lot of pain in life.

So where do evil people go? If you had to make a list of all the places you should probably avoid, what would make the list? Certain parties? Certain houses? Certain businesses?

Sometimes it's a matter of keeping your eyes wide open. Ask God to show you who to avoid and what to avoid. (He will, if you ask.)

Refuse to go where the wicked go. Refuse to do what the wicked do. Refuse to say what the wicked say. Refuse to watch what the wicked watch. Refuse to talk the way the wicked talk.

You have the power inside you to refuse all of that. When you don't (when you give in and start acting like the wicked act), problems rise up like mountains in front of you! They're insurmountable.

Avoid the mountains by avoiding the people, places, and things that stand in opposition to God. He has better things for you than all that!

I'll avoid evil people, Lord. And I'll stay out of the
places they go. Thank You for reminding me that I can
have the courage to refuse all of it. Amen.

What They Think of You

It is dangerous to be concerned with what others think of you, but if you trust the LORD, you are safe.
PROVERBS 29:25 GNT

How much time do you spend fretting over what other people think of you? How you look. How you act. How you dress. How you wear your hair. How you speak. How you study. How talented you are. . .or aren't.

If you're like most girls, you probably spend way too much time worrying about the impression you're making (or not making) on those you hope to impress. But why? Why does it matter so much what they think? So that you can belong to a certain circle of friends? So that you can be popular? So that you can get attention?

We all want to be loved. That's a universal need. But things can get a little crazy if you hyperfocus on what others are thinking. What really matters is what God thinks. (And what your parents and teachers think is pretty important too.) Do your best not to focus on what your peers think. Will it really matter a year from now? Or two years? Or ten?

Focus on eternal things, the things that will matter not just this week or this year, but years from now. Those are the important things.

I'll focus on what's important, not what makes me popular, Jesus. Help me keep my eyes on the prize. . .You! Amen.

The Mountain of Emotions

Jesus wept.
JOHN 11:35 ESV

Aren't you glad this tiny verse is in the Bible? It's the shortest Bible verse, and yet it contains a vast wealth of information about our Savior.

Jesus felt stuff. Really, truly felt stuff. Maybe you think about Him as some impersonal faraway God, one who doesn't "get" the stuff you're going through. But when Jesus' friend Lazarus died, He cried.

There are a bunch of theories about why He cried. Some would say it was because He missed His friend. Others might argue that Jesus was upset because people didn't trust that He would take care of things. Regardless, He cried. He cared. In fact, He cared so much that He leaked tears out of His eyes.

Think about that the next time you're upset to the point of crying. If you start to think, *God doesn't care*, remember. . .He's been there too. He wept. He agonized. And He understands your pain and anguish, far more than you think He does.

***

Jesus, thank You for the reminder that You care! You lost Your friend and Your heart broke. I've been through heartbreak too, and I've felt so alone. It helps to know that You get it! You've walked a mile in my shoes. Thank You for caring so deeply about what I go through. Amen.

A Time for Everything

...a time to cry and a time to laugh, a time
to mourn and a time to dance.
ECCLESIASTES 3:4 GW

According to the third chapter of Ecclesiastes (a book in the Old Testament), there's a time for all of the emotions. There's a time to cry. (Hey, sometimes you can't help yourself!) There's a time to laugh. (Thank goodness, right? If life was all about crying, you'd be in a lot of trouble!)

There's a time to mourn. Hard times will come. You can count on it. But there's also a time to celebrate with dance.

In other words, there will be good days and bad. There will be happy times and sad. There will be days when you're dancing for joy and other days when you wonder if anyone even knows you're alive.

It's so good to know that God sees us and cares on all those days. He's not just there when things are going well. He's in the depths of the pain when we're at the end of ourselves. And He's celebrating alongside us when joyous seasons come. He's a God who participates in it all—good and bad.

Jesus, I'm so glad for the reminder that You're with
me all of my days. No matter what I'm feeling, I give
my emotions—and my life—to You. Amen.

Authenticity

A glad heart makes a happy face; a broken heart crushes the spirit.
<small>PROVERBS 15:13 NLT</small>

Maybe you've heard the phrase "Fake it till you make it." Sounds reasonable, right? Only, what happens when you reach the point where you can't fake it anymore? (We all reach that point inevitably.)

You can force your face into a smile, but the icky stuff going on inside of your heart won't allow that smile to stick for long. As soon as you turn away from the crowd, your lips tip back downward into a frown.

God would prefer authenticity. Face the mountains in front of you—the broken heart, the sadness, the struggles. Speak to them. Watch them fall.

In other words, deal with the heart issues. Don't let them consume you. Don't pretend to be okay when you're not. Don't hide your struggles from others.

Get real. Get vulnerable. Face the mountains and speak to them, then allow Jesus to heal your heart—totally and completely.

I get so tired of faking it, Jesus. I plaster on a smile and pretend everything is okay, even when it's not. This is no way to live. Help me be more vulnerable so that I can be healed. I want to knock these mountains down in Jesus' name! Amen.

Feel Their Pain, Share Their Joy

Rejoice with those who rejoice, weep with those who weep.
ROMANS 12:15 ESV

Have you ever heard the word *empath*? An empath is someone who feels the pain of others. Let's face it—some people are more empathetic than others. (Some people don't seem to notice or care when others are hurting. That stinks!)

God calls you to be an empath. He wants you to notice when that girl next to you is having a bad day. He also wants you to be available to celebrate with that friend who just got terrific news, even if it happens to be on a day when everything is going wrong for you.

And what about the really hard stuff, like when your best friend's mom is going through cancer treatment or your neighbor is in the hospital? Pay attention, girl! Be there for those who are facing mountains of their own. Your prayers can play a role in knocking those mountains down. And your presence (and kind, thoughtful words) will be just what the doctor ordered to soothe troubled souls.

Show up. Pay attention. Feel what others feel. In other words, love them as Jesus loves them.

I want to be You with skin on, Jesus! I want to represent You well as I love others. Show me how to rejoice with those who are rejoicing and mourn with those who mourn. Amen.

A Rope of Three Cords

*Two people can resist an attack that would defeat one person
alone. A rope made of three cords is hard to break.*
ECCLESIASTES 4:12 GNT

Have you ever tried to fight a battle alone? Can you even imagine a warrior going to battle without his fellow warriors on his right and left? It's much harder to win when you're facing the bad guys all by yourself. And let's face it—having someone with you makes you more courageous. There is definitely power in numbers!

Think of that truth in light of today's verse. If someone handed you a rope and said, "Use this to climb down the side of a ten-story building," you would probably check the strength of the rope's strands, right?

Life is a lot like that ten-story building. It's filled with dangers at every turn. And the people God has placed around you. . .they're your rope. When you try to go it alone, you've got a one-stranded rope. You'll crash and burn if you try to scale a building with that!

Don't crash and burn, girl. Grab hold of the people around you and ask them to face the mountains alongside you. You'll do great things for God as long as you stick together.

---

*Thank You for the prayer warriors in my life, Jesus!
I don't know what I'd do without them! They are my
threefold cord, and I'm so grateful for them. Amen.*

Self-Control: Use It, Don't Lose It!

A man without self-control is like a city
broken into and left without walls.
PROVERBS 25:28 ESV

Self-control is like the brakes on your car. If you didn't have brakes, well. . .that drive wouldn't end well, would it?

Maybe this is why so many of your relationships end with mountains instead of peaceful valleys. Maybe your lack of self-control is causing problems with some of the people in your circle.

What does a lack of self-control look like? It's demanding. It always has to have its own way. It says, "I'm going to do it anyway, even if I'm not supposed to." It doesn't worry about consequences.

If you have a lack of self-control, you'll end up in all sorts of trouble. People who can't exhibit control don't just take one drink of alcohol. . .they end up drinking to excess. And it's the same no matter what bad action one takes—cheating, cussing, hanging out with the wrong people. When you have no self-control, you do it all to excess without worrying about how the story will end.

God is concerned about how your story ends, so start using the self-control He gave you, girl! Put the brakes on the car before you drive over a cliff!

Show me how to use the self-control You've given me,
Lord Jesus! I want to live a controlled, secure life! Amen.

Out to Impress?

*Don't be selfish; don't try to impress others. Be humble,
thinking of others as better than yourselves.*
PHILIPPIANS 2:3 NLT

Have you ever met someone who was always out to impress others? Maybe he loved to talk about his own talents or abilities. Maybe she was always showing off her dance moves or gymnastic skills.

It's hard not to show off when you've got skills. But on the other hand, it's good to let other people shine. Sometimes we cause mountains to rise up in relationships just because we like to turn the spotlight on ourselves.

It's easy to do, isn't it? Maybe you find yourself bragging about your report card or carrying on about how the science teacher said you're her favorite. Maybe you can't help but sing at the top of your lungs after someone tells you that you have a nice voice.

There's nothing wrong with using your gifts. Just make sure you give others a chance to shine too. Don't hog the spotlight, girl! You've got special talents and abilities, sure, but so do lots of other people in your circle.

$\longrightarrow$

*Show me how to be humble like You, Jesus. I don't want to be known
as a show-off. Please help me keep my attitude and actions in check
so that I'm not always out to impress. (That can get so old!) Amen.*

A Cloud of Witnesses

*Therefore, since we are surrounded by so great a cloud of witnesses,
let us also lay aside every weight, and sin which clings so closely,
and let us run with endurance the race that is set before us.*

<small>HEBREWS 12:1 ESV</small>

Today's verse says that we are surrounded by a cloud of witnesses. What in the world does that mean?

Think about the mighty men and women from Bible times. Moses had to travel across the desert and lead a host of Israelites to the Promised Land. David had to fight Goliath. Joshua saw the walls fall down at Jericho. Jonah got swallowed by a big fish. Joseph was thrown into a pit.

These folks saw some action. And yet they all went on to do great things for God!

Think of them as football fans in a stadium, filling every seat. You're on the field, playing your heart out. And they're rising to their feet shouting, "Go, girl! If I could do it, you can! If I could fight that lion, you can fight your battle!" "If I could make it across the Red Sea, you can make it through this valley you're walking through!" "If I could see the walls of Jericho fall, you can see the mountains in front of you tumble to the ground!"

Let their testimonies be an encouragement to you. They're in the stands even now, ready to cheer you on!

$$\Longrightarrow$$

*Thank You for the reminder that many people have already
faced the obstacles I'm now facing, Jesus. . .and then
some! What a great cloud of witnesses! Amen.*

The Best One Is Love

So these three things remain: faith, hope, and
love. But the best one of these is love.
1 Corinthians 13:13 gw

Love is the greatest gift God ever gave you. It's like a rare jewel—priceless, even. When you have love, you have everything you need.

What good would it do you to overcome every obstacle in your life, to see every mountain fall, if you didn't love people? Sure, you could brag about all the great things God had done for you, but your words would fall on deaf ears if you weren't treating people well.

Without love, nothing else works. It's like gasoline in a car. You won't make it very far without gas, will you? Same with love. It's the missing ingredient. It's the sugar in the cake, the yeast in the bread, the oil in the lamp.

Faith is important. It helps you overcome troubles.

Hope is important. It will keep you going when you don't feel like it (especially when you're facing hard times).

But love? It's truly the one thing that rises to the top, the reason you were put on this planet—to love God and love people! How are you doing with that, girl?

I love You, Lord God. . .and I love people! I want to do better
at this love thing, though. Help me, I pray. Amen.

Do What He Says

*"If you love me, keep my commands. And I will ask the
Father, and he will give you another advocate to help
you and be with you forever—the Spirit of truth."*
JOHN 14:15–17 NIV

"If you love me, you'll do what I say." Maybe you've heard a parent speak these words. They're not trying to be manipulative. They really mean it. Love is followed by action.

The Bible is full of if/then verses. If we do our part, then God does His part. But we have to do the *if*.

Often we wonder why God doesn't come through for us. We feel betrayed. Then, after some time has passed, we come to understand that we were the ones who didn't do our part. We didn't do the *if*.

If you love God, then follow His Word. Stick to it even when it's hard. Do the right thing even if no one else around you is. (It's hard, but not impossible.)

If you will do this, your victories will increase! Amazing things will happen, and all as a result of your simple obedience. Best of all, you will be honoring the Lord.

———›››———————→

*I want to honor You by doing what You've called me to do,
Jesus. I love You. . .so I'll do what You say! Amen.*

His Ways Are Different

*"My thoughts," says the LORD, "are not like yours,
and my ways are different from yours."*
ISAIAH 55:8 GNT

Have you ever wondered what the Lord is thinking? Is He sitting up in heaven right now, thinking of you? Or is He focused on the war going on across the globe? Maybe He's busy taking care of those kids in the third-world country who have no food. Or maybe He's in the process of healing someone who has cancer.

Here's the cool thing about the King of kings and Lord of lords: He's doing all those things at this very moment. He's capable of doing all things at once. You'll never fully comprehend what He's doing, and neither will you understand what He's thinking.

God's ways are different from ours. His thoughts are different from ours. And even though we're created in His image, He's so far above us that we stand in awe of who He is and all He does.

———→

Lord, You are magnificent! Your thoughts are too lofty for me! I can't figure You out, but I'm so grateful for all that You're doing, even now as I whisper this prayer. You're healing, You're encouraging, You're bringing peace to shattered hearts. I can't do any of that, but I can pray to the one who can. And I can watch You tear down mountains with just a word. I'm so grateful, Jesus! Amen.

Be Led by the Spirit

Those who are dominated by the sinful nature think about sinful things, but those who are controlled by the Holy Spirit think about things that please the Spirit. So letting your sinful nature control your mind leads to death. But letting the Spirit control your mind leads to life and peace.

ROMANS 8:5–6 NLT

When you read the phrase "dominated by the sinful nature," what images come to mind? We are born into a broken, fallen world. It's not really in our nature to follow after God. We're more inclined to do the wrong thing than the right one.

But when we allow ourselves to become "dominated" by bad decisions, we're in deep, deep trouble. In many ways we're like that addict who can't say no to the next drink because he's chemically addicted. We're trapped.

God knew about this sort of trap, of course. And He made a plan for us to escape it! When Jesus ascended into heaven, He sent us the Holy Spirit. The Spirit lives inside of each believer, offering discernment—the ability to tell right from wrong.

Want to avoid some of the mountains in your life? Listen to the Holy Spirit and follow His lead. Even now He's giving you the ability to choose the right things. Don't let your sinful nature take control. Escape the trap. Be led by the Spirit into a life of peace, one where mountains tumble to dust at the mention of Jesus' name!

I won't be trapped, Lord. I won't allow myself to be dominated by my sinful nature. I refuse to be controlled by the enemy. Thank You for setting me free by Your Spirit! May I live this way. . .forever! Amen.

Be Transformed

Do not be conformed to this world, but be transformed by the renewal of your mind, that by testing you may discern what is the will of God, what is good and acceptable and perfect.

ROMANS 12:2 ESV

Have you ever watched a cake decorator at work? Oftentimes she (or he) is called on to make decorative pieces out of fondant, which is kind of like an edible playdough. She reaches for her favorite molds and presses the fondant inside. Then out pops a flower. Or a dinosaur. Or a baby bootie. The fondant takes on the shape of whatever the mold happens to be.

Jesus is like a fondant mold. You are like the fondant (the playdough). He wants you to be transformed into His image. Press yourself close to Him, then watch as the shape of your life begins to look more and more like Jesus!

Don't press yourself into the world's mold. It's a false one, for sure. You won't look the way God intends. You won't be as effective. And you'll end up facing a zillion mountains that didn't have to be. Instead, fully allow yourself—heart, mind, and soul—to be transformed (changed) into His image.

How do you do this? Start by giving Him your thoughts. Say, "Lord God, please renew my mind!" When you do that, you will begin to think like Him. And eventually your actions will follow.

→

I get it, Lord Jesus. I want to be more like You. Today I press close to You. Form me into Your image, I pray. Amen.

Speak It!

For the word of God is alive and active. Sharper than any double-edged sword, it penetrates even to dividing soul and spirit, joints and marrow; it judges the thoughts and attitudes of the heart.
HEBREWS 4:12 NIV

Are you standing at the base of a gigantic mountain, wondering if it will ever come crashing down? Speak the Word.

Are you facing a relationship problem so big that you don't know if your friend will ever speak to you again? Speak the Word.

Are you facing a health crisis, a true life-and-death situation? Speak the Word.

When you speak the words of the Bible out loud, you are putting God's words into your own mouth. Then, as they're spoken, you're releasing them out loud for the enemy to hear. He craters once he hears the Word of God. He runs like a sniveling coward at the mention of the name of Jesus, so use the words that Jesus spoke. Speak the words that were in His mouth. Those words are powerful. They're sharp like a knife. They're battle ready. They will do what you alone cannot do.

Speak the Word. It will change everything.

———————⟫⟫⟫———————→

I will speak Your Word, Jesus. I'll memorize scriptures to use for every battle. Put them on my tongue, I pray. They will be sharp and powerful, ready to come to my defense! Amen.

Strength to Keep Going

He gives power to the weak and strength to the powerless.
Even youths will become weak and tired, and young men
will fall in exhaustion. But those who trust in the LORD will
find new strength. They will soar high on wings like eagles.
They will run and not grow weary. They will walk and not faint.
ISAIAH 40:29–31 NLT

Everyone gets weary. Everyone says, "I can't keep going." Whether you're young or old, you'll crash and burn if you overextend yourself or if life gets crazy. Hey, it happens.

But look at today's passage. At the very same time you're saying, "I just can't!" God is whispering, "Yep, you can!" And then He's zapping you with supernatural strength and energy to get the tasks done.

There are going to be days where it's all Him and not you. . .at all. You'll look back on those days and say, "Whoa. I can tell that was Jesus at work, not me! I was a basket case that day!"

Maybe today is a basket case day. That's okay. Even today, when you're tired and weary, even when you're stumbling and falling all over the place, God is still renewing your strength. You will soar like an eagle today. Read that again. You can—and will—soar like an eagle today. You'll keep running, even when you don't feel like it. And you'll make it to the end of the day, surprised and delighted that God somehow brought you through.

He will renew (make new) your strength. Trust Him.

$\longrightarrow$

I trust You, Jesus, even on the days when I feel like I have no energy
to keep going. Thank You for renewing my strength! Amen.

Don't Beat Yourself Up!

*There is therefore now no condemnation
for those who are in Christ Jesus.*

ROMANS 8:1 ESV

Do you ever beat yourself up? Maybe you decide to eat more veggies but end up eating a giant slice of cake instead. Or two. Or three. Afterward, you can't stop thinking about what a loser you are. Why can't you get your act together? Why are you so flawed?

Or maybe you promise yourself you won't snap at your mom when she asks you to do something around the house. Only, you blow it. You react in an ugly way to her. You see the pain in her eyes, but you can't seem to help yourself. Then, afterward, you beat yourself up because you know it was all so unnecessary and wrong.

God wants you to be accountable for the things you do wrong, but once you've asked for His forgiveness (and repented to those you've hurt), it's over, girl. There's no need to replay it in your mind.

The mountain of condemnation is a huge one, and the enemy knows just how to mess you up with it. Don't let him. Leave the past in the past. You've been forgiven and set free. There's no need to go on beating yourself up. Just continue to walk in the forgiveness and grace that Jesus offered when He died on the cross for you.

*Whew! I'm over it, Jesus. I'm done beating myself up.
Thank You for the reminder that I don't have to live like that.
I'm so grateful for Your grace and forgiveness. Amen.*

Precious Jewels

How precious to me are your thoughts,
O God! How vast is the sum of them!
PSALM 139:17 ESV

Imagine your grandmother has a collection of beautiful rubies. She has rings, earrings, necklaces, and even bracelets. You love going over to her house to look at the jewels, which she's happy to show off every time.

Now imagine she tells you that she's planning to leave all those rubies to you when she passes away. You would be overwhelmed, no doubt! To think that those rubies might be yours one day is too much to fathom.

In some ways, God's thoughts are like those rubies. They're precious jewels. And even though they don't belong to us now, we can be assured of the fact that they are there for our good. He's thinking good thoughts about us, in other words.

His thoughts are worth far more than jewels, for sure. The same God who thought of zebras and daffodils, cumulus clouds and rainbows, is also thinking about you. Right now. In this very moment. And His thoughts are for your good, not for evil.

How precious, God's thoughts! And how He loves you, His daughter!

>>>———————→

Thanks for thinking of me, Lord! It makes me smile to think
I'm on Your mind. You're on my mind too! Amen.

A Brand-New You

*So get rid of your old self, which made you live as you used to—
the old self that was being destroyed by its deceitful desires.
Your hearts and minds must be made completely new, and you
must put on the new self, which is created in God's likeness
and reveals itself in the true life that is upright and holy.*
EPHESIANS 4:22–24 GNT

Have you ever seen one of those infomercials (or social media ads) that promised a brand-new you? Maybe the ad says something like this: "30 Days to a Brand-New You!" Maybe the ad goes on to promise you can drop twenty pounds in a week or have shinier hair if you use a certain shampoo. Or maybe some product promises to clear up the pimples on your face, if you just spend $69.95 to buy it.

Starting over is always fun and exciting. . .at first. Keeping it up isn't so easy! Think of that in light of today's verse: God promises—truly promises—that you can get rid of your old self. He's not talking about your weight. Or your hair. Or even changes to your personality. God is interested in dealing with your sinful state and all the icky desires that go with it.

You can have a new you. . .one that is complete and whole in Jesus. Now, that's a worthwhile new beginning!

→

*I'm ready to start over with You, Jesus! I want a brand-
new me, so please work on my heart to draw me closer to
You. May I become more like You in every way! Amen.*

Set Your Mind on Things Above

Set your minds on things that are above,
not on things that are on earth.
COLOSSIANS 3:2 ESV

Have you ever said the words "Just don't think about it!"? Maybe you're facing something hard and you would rather think about anything else.

It really is possible to push your thoughts away, but they never stay away for long, do they? Before long, you're back to fretting as you stare at that mountain looming in front of you.

There's a solution to this problem. You can give that mountain to Jesus. You can ask Him to take hold of your thoughts and calm you down. You can set your mind on things above.

Think of it this way: You have some keys in your hand. You can set them down on the table, where someone might knock them off, or you can hang them up high on the hook. You choose to hang them up high.

That's kind of what it's like to set your mind on things above. You won't be fretting over what's going on below because someone much higher is in control. The things of this earth will pass away, but God's ways will last throughout all eternity. Give it to Him. Set your mind on Him.

⟫⟶

I get it, Jesus. I don't have to be hyperfocused on
this world or the problems I'm facing while I'm here.
I can set my mind on You instead. Amen.

Puzzling Things

*Trust in the LORD with all your heart, and do
not lean on your own understanding.*
PROVERBS 3:5 ESV

"I just don't get it."

No doubt you've used those words a time or two. There are so many puzzling things in this life, after all. Crazy things happen, and we can't always make sense of them. (Hey, that's partly because we live in a fallen world. We're not in heaven yet!)

It's hard to trust in God when things don't make sense. There's no pretending this faith journey is always easy. But doing your best to lean on His understanding—and not your own—will help.

You won't get it. A lot. But He gets it every time. He sees every side of every situation. He sees today. . .and tomorrow. He sees the motivations and the schemes of the enemy. And most of all, He adores you and is for you. He's on your team.

So don't give up when things don't make sense. Don't throw up your hands and say, "Forget all of this! I'm out!"

Don't check out. Just lean into Him and watch as He performs a miracle once again, sweeping those crazy mountains you're facing into the sea.

*I don't get it, Jesus. I could write a book of all the things
I don't understand. But You do. You see it all and You
care. Thank You for loving me so much and for teaching
me how to lean into You when I don't get it. Amen.*

All Things

We know that all things work together for the good of those who love God—those whom he has called according to his plan.
ROMANS 8:28 GW

How many things work together for good in your life? The great things? The exciting things? The "I can't believe how lucky I am!" things?

No, all things. Even the "Why did that have to happen to my family?" things. And the "Why did I fail that test?" things. And the "I can't believe she passed away—I'm going to miss her so much" things.

All things work together for good for those who love God and are called according to His plan. So does He love you? Of course He does! Has He called you to be a part of a bigger plan? You betcha!

You can know for sure that He's going to work everything together for good. Those mountains in front of you, the ones casting crazy-large shadows down on you even now? He'll work those for good. That pain you've been experiencing, the grief and the heartache? Even those will be woven into the beautiful tapestry of your life story, the one that (by the way) He can and will use to bring others into the kingdom.

Hang on, girl. He's working it out.

———————

Thank You for changing the story from bad to good, Jesus. I know I can trust You to turn things around, even on the worst day. You'll use it as part of my life story, my testimony. I put my faith in You. Amen.

What Kind of Seeds Are You Planting?

And those who are peacemakers will plant seeds of
peace and reap a harvest of righteousness.
JAMES 3:18 NLT

You're a seed planter, whether you realize it or not. Every day you're dropping seeds all along the path. Sometimes weeds spring up. Other times beautiful flowers break through the soil. What you produce is totally up to you.

So how does this work, exactly? When you speak words of life, peace, joy, and hope, you're planting beautiful flowers. When you get angry and worked up, when you cause division and mistrust between friends, you're breeding weeds.

You know the problem with weeds, right? Before long they grow so big that they strangle the rest of the plants in the garden. They take over.

That's why it's important to stop the bad seeds before they hit the ground. You can choose, even in the very moment, to speak words of life. You can make a deliberate effort to make things better, not worse.

You can plant flowers. And when you do, you leave behind a wonderful aroma, pleasing to all. But when you drop bad seeds, those weeds take over.

You choose. Good seeds or bad?

I want to plant good seeds, Jesus. With my words. With my actions.
With my attitude. I don't want to be responsible for anything negative
or bad. I don't want to cause problems for others. Help me as I
go through my day to honor You with the seeds I drop. Amen.

It's Coming

*"The vision will still happen at the appointed time.
It hurries toward its goal. It won't be a lie. If it's delayed,
wait for it. It will certainly happen. It won't be late."*
HABAKKUK 2:3 GW

If God said it, it will happen. He told Moses that the Israelites would reach the Promised Land. . .and they did. He told Hannah that she would have a child. . .and she did. He told Isaiah—hundreds of years before Christ was born—that He was sending a Savior to Bethlehem, one who would be led as a lamb to the slaughter. . .and He did.

God doesn't go back on His word. He's a keeper of promises. There has never been one instance in the history of the world when He didn't follow through.

Sometimes His promises seem delayed. Maybe your family has been waiting on a miracle and it hasn't come yet. Keep waiting. He's still in the miracle-working business. And the cool thing about God is this—it might seem late to You, but He's always right on time.

Trust Him in the waiting. If He said it. . .

Well, you know the rest. You can trust Him, girl.

⫸⟶

*I will trust You even in the waiting, Jesus. You've promised that the
appointed time is coming. It's hurrying toward its goal. I'll keep waiting
for it even if it seems delayed. I believe it's on the way. Amen.*

The Secret to Happiness

I know how to get along with little and how to live when I have much.
I have learned the secret of being happy at all times. If I am full of
food and have all I need, I am happy. If I am hungry and need more,
I am happy. I can do all things because Christ gives me the strength.
PHILIPPIANS 4:12–13 NLV

Human beings are fickle, aren't they? We celebrate when things go our way, then gripe and complain when they don't. We forget that God is still on the throne when mountains rise up in front of us. (Why do we forget all the awesome things He's done for us in the past? Those things should encourage us!)

Check out today's verse: "I know how to get along with little and how to live when I have much." Can you say that and mean it—*really* mean it? Chances are pretty good you prefer to have much. Much money. Much clothes. Much food. Much friends. Much popularity. Much talent.

We're addicted to the "much," aren't we? But we have to learn how to be content when we're going through the lean times. If we can't learn to thank God for the "little," then maybe He'll wait a little longer to give us the much!

Lord, I want to honor You no matter what the situation looks like—
little or much. I know the secret of being happy. I can do all things
through You because You give me strength no matter what!

Seek Him First

*"But seek first the kingdom of God and his righteousness,
and all these things will be added to you."*
MATTHEW 6:33 ESV

What's the first thing? The most important thing? The one thing? If someone asked you, "What's literally the most important thing in your life right now?" how would you answer?

One of the reasons you face mountains in your life is because your "one thing" is off. You're focused on ten thousand things, but they're out of order. Put Jesus first and everything else falls into place. He's the one thing. If you're hoping for all the other things, you'll have to go on hoping until you finally figure this out.

Want friends? Put Jesus first.

Want to grow your talents and abilities? Put Jesus first.

Want to get control of your diet and exercise? Put Jesus first.

When you place Him in His rightful place on the throne of your life, all these things will be added to you. That's a promise from Jesus Himself. But if you don't put Him in His right place, you'll be waiting a long, long time. . .until you eventually seek Him first.

Stop slowing the process, girl. Put Him first!

→

*Sometimes I get off course, Jesus! I put my grades first. Or my
friends. Or my activities. Sometimes I even put church ahead of You.
Then I wonder why I have mountains in front of me. From now on,
You'll get the top spot! Help me remember to seek You first. Amen.*

Who Are You Imitating?

Therefore be imitators of God, as beloved children.
EPHESIANS 5:1 ESV

Have you ever played Follow the Leader? It's fun as a game. But in real life? Not so much. Following after people will usually get you in trouble.

If you're going to imitate anyone, let it be God, not your friends. Sure, there will be a few you want to be like. You might even be a little envious of some of the more talented ones or more spiritual ones. But in the end, chase after the only leader who counts: Jesus.

Think about His disciples. They were ordinary men with ordinary jobs. Some were fishermen. One was a tax collector. But they left everything to follow after Jesus. They didn't look to one another for answers. They looked only to Him.

That's how it should be with you too. You have a great friend group. There are some terrific godly people in your circle. And you do need to draw close to them and learn from them. But when it comes to who you imitate? Let it be Christ and Christ alone!

>>>———————→

*I want to be more like You, Jesus! Thank You for the
friends You've given me. I've learned so much from them.
But ultimately it's You I want to follow! Amen.*

Seated in Heavenly Places

"Those who are victorious will sit with me on my throne,
just as I was victorious and sat with my Father on his throne."
REVELATION 3:21 NLT

Have you ever considered the fact that you're not just an overcomer? You're not just a mover of mountains. This life of faith you're living right now will have an eternal payoff! Jesus says that one day the overcomers (that's you!) will sit with Him on His throne.

Whoa.

That's a lot to absorb, isn't it? The idea of sitting alongside the King of kings and Lord of lords for all eternity? Right there, so close you could touch Him?

Seems too much to imagine!

Yet that's what He says. . .and that's what He means. Victory has a lovely payoff in the end. So go on knocking over mountains. Go on speaking in faith. Go on looking your obstacles in the eye and saying, "Get lost. . .in Jesus' name!"

Jesus, it's so cool to think that one day I'll sit side by
side with You. I can't wait for the promise of heaven.
Watching You rule and reign is going to be amazing! Amen.

You're Already Won

But you belong to God, my dear children. You have already
won a victory over those people, because the Spirit who lives
in you is greater than the spirit who lives in the world.

1 John 4:4 nlt

You've already won.

Read those words again. In faith, your mountain has already moved. You see it directly in front of you, but your faith is already casting it into the sea.

So how do you move forward when you realize Jesus has already won the battle? First of all, you relax. You don't stress out all the time. You trust that when He said, "It is finished," that awful day on the cross, it really was. And is.

The crisis in front of you: it's finished.

The health problem you're facing: He has won that victory.

The relationship woes you're struggling through: you've already won those battles too.

Here's the truth: Jesus paid it all (and did it all) on the cross over two thousand years ago. When He said, "It is finished," He really meant it. He knew the battles were already won.

Do you?

I know it now, Jesus! You've won every battle, and I'm so grateful.
I put my total trust in You for the mountains in front of me.
I'm already calling their bluff. They're done, in Jesus' name! Amen.

No Eternal Sting

"O death, where is your victory? O death, where is your sting?"
The sting of death is sin, and the power of sin is the law. But thanks
be to God, who gives us the victory through our Lord Jesus Christ.
1 CORINTHIANS 15:55–57 ESV

When you hear the words *He died*, what goes through your mind? Are you overwhelmed by the idea of death? Does it seem like the biggest mountain of all, one to be feared?

When you're young, losing people can feel catastrophic. The older you get, the more your thoughts on death seem to change. Instead of fearing their mortality, elderly people often reconcile themselves to the idea that they will be in heaven soon.

Does this seem strange to you? Probably, since you're young. But remember today's verse. Jesus wants you to know that there's no eternal "sting" (think bee sting) where death is concerned. It hurts for a minute, like when you're first stung. But if you're the one who has died, and if you're a believer, you're entering eternity with the King of kings! There's no sting in that, is there?

Don't be afraid when you hear that a believing loved one has died. You will see that sweet person again. Give your heart to Jesus, and you'll spend all eternity with them. . .and with Him.

⟫⟫⟫———————→

I trust You, Jesus, even with the hardest mountain of all. . .death.
Teach me to have an eternal perspective. Amen.

Strongholds Must Go

For the weapons of our warfare are not of the flesh but have divine power to destroy strongholds. We destroy arguments and every lofty opinion raised against the knowledge of God, and take every thought captive to obey Christ, being ready to punish every disobedience, when your obedience is complete.
2 Corinthians 10:4–6 esv

Whoa. Those are some powerful weapons you have in your arsenal, girl! Talk about being equipped! You are. . .and then some! And what effective weapons you have. Today's verse says that the weapons Jesus has given you have divine power to destroy strongholds.

So what is a stronghold? It's anything that has held you in its grip. Like jealousy. Or bitterness. Or overeating. Or anger.

No matter how strong the hold, the weapons you have are stronger. You can take your thoughts captive. (That's where most mountains start, after all—in your mind.) You can stop them before they blow up into something big.

Use the weapons the Lord has given you. Don't just assume these strongholds will never go away. They can be gone today, in Jesus' name. Speak to those mountains, girl!

I speak to the strongholds in my life in the name of Jesus. You have to flee! You have no power over me. I'm a daughter of the Most High King! Amen.

Endure to the End

*"And many false prophets will arise and lead many astray.
And because lawlessness will be increased, the love of many
will grow cold. But the one who endures to the end will be saved."*
MATTHEW 24:11–13 ESV

There's a lot of crazy talk out there. People who used to be strong in their faith are falling for all kinds of things! You have to be on your guard because the enemy of your soul wants to convince you that the Bible is no longer relevant and that the instructions inside of that great book aren't really for today.

Wrong! And even if the one spreading that message claims to be in ministry, you're wiser than that. You know a false prophet when you see one. You're going to see their false teaching for what it is. (False prophets throw up mountains all over the place. . .on purpose! They're trying to distract you from the truth of God!)

Endure to the end. Stay true to what the Bible says. It's not going to be easy. People these days don't like some of the things they find in the Word of God. You, though? You're not going to give up on the Bible, no matter what.

*I won't give up on Your Word, Jesus. It contains the message of
salvation and can change the life of even the most lost person! Amen.*

Powered from the Inside Out!

*I have been crucified with Christ. It is no longer I who live,
but Christ who lives in me. And the life I now live in the flesh I live
by faith in the Son of God, who loved me and gave himself for me.*
GALATIANS 2:20 ESV

What does it mean to be crucified with Christ? Is this verse saying that when Jesus died, you died too?

Here's the truth: when you give your heart to Him, you are dead to your old self. You literally put to death the "old man" (the old you, in other words).

You don't want the icky old stuff from the past to affect your future, so you get rid of it once and for all. (Hey, those mountains of yesterday are no more! They no longer have power over you!)

The life you're living right now is a life of faith, not a life filled with selfish ambitions. Jesus poured Himself out for you, and now you're pouring yourself out for Him. He lives inside of you, which means you're now getting your power from the inside out!

*I live in Your power, not my own, Jesus! You've put those
old habits to rest once and for all. Now You're living in
me, calling the shots and giving me the tools I need to say
no to the harmful things. I'm so grateful. Amen.*

Don't Get Trapped

*For the LORD will be your confidence and will
keep your foot from being caught.*
PROVERBS 3:26 ESV

Have you ever seen a trapper lay a trap in the forest? He puts it down, hoping the animal will happen by and step into it. When that happens, the trap closes, locking down on the animal's foot and holding it in place.

Sounds painful. . .and horrible!

The enemy of your soul likes to think he's a great trapper. He lays all sorts of traps in your path, hoping you'll happen by. When you step into them, you feel caught, like there's no way out.

Only, you're not! Look at today's verse. God will be your confidence. You can walk without fear that you're about to get trapped. He will keep your foot from being caught.

You can trust Him. Those old traps—the things that used to trip you up? They're not a bother anymore. Those were old mountains that have long since disappeared. You're a new person now, a child of the King. He's got you!

———————⟫⟫⟫———————→

*My foot won't be caught, Jesus! I won't give in to the enemy's
traps. I have You on my side now, and that's all I need. Amen.*

He Is Exalted!

"Be still, and know that I am God. I will be exalted
among the nations, I will be exalted in the earth!"
Psalm 46:10 esv

Why do you suppose God is in the mountain-moving business? He could leave those obstacles in our paths for us to deal with on our own, after all. Some people might even argue that we deserve troubles because we lead such sinful lives.

God adores us. We're His children. And when we call on Him, He's quick to answer—He loves to move on our behalf. But there's another reason He still performs miracles today. Whenever He moves in a miraculous way, He is exalted. He's lifted up. People notice. They point to where the mountain used to be and say things like, "Whoa! God really came through for you, didn't He?"

The miracle is undeniably God's doing. It points right back to Him. And imagine this: at the very same moment He's moving a mountain for you, He's moving mountains for thousands—possibly even millions—of other people across the globe. That's a lot of miracles all taking place at once. Imagine how many lives are being changed!

Thank You for moving in such miraculous ways, Jesus! I pray
that people all over the earth see what You're up to! Amen.

You Know It in Your Knower

My heart is confident in you, O God; my heart is confident. No wonder I can sing your praises!
PSALM 57:7 NLT

Sometimes you just know things. You know them in your knower. People ask, "How do you know for sure?" and you just shrug. There's no doubt in your mind. You're confident.

Confidence is a good thing, as long as you first place your trust in Jesus. When you do that, He gives you a holy confidence to know what to do and when to do it. He builds you up from the inside out. Doubts disappear as faith and courage rise up. You step out boldly when you know that you know that you know you're moving in the right direction.

So how confident are you? Maybe you're one of those girls who feels unsure of herself a lot of the time. Start by putting your full faith and trust in the Lord. When you know who you are in Him and when you're convinced of His great love for you, you will learn to trust that He's working everything out on your behalf. And when you have that kind of trust, your confidence will grow! Then all those decisions you have to make will be a breeze.

My confidence is in You, Jesus. I'm so glad I don't have to put my trust in anyone or anything else. Amen.

Rejoice in the Waiting

*Rejoice in our confident hope. Be patient in
trouble, and keep on praying.*
ROMANS 12:12 NLT

Would you consider yourself a patient person? How are you at waiting? If someone said, "I'm going to give you ten thousand dollars, but you have to wait a year to get it," how would you handle that year?

Waiting isn't easy. And when you're staring at mountains in front of you, the wait can seem like an eternity. Even if you feel in your spirit that God has promised to knock down those mountains, you might get depressed at how long it takes to actually happen.

God isn't on our timetable. His concept of time is completely different from ours. Maybe this is why we're told in Romans 12:12 to rejoice in our confident hope. To be patient in trouble and keep on praying. Maybe the Lord gave us these instructions because He realizes how impatient we are, how quick we are to give up.

Don't give up. Keep on rejoicing, even when you don't feel like it. Keep on praying, even when troubles come.

Patience, girl. It's a virtue He wants you to have.

*I'll be patient, Lord. I'll keep waiting. And praying.
And believing. . .no matter how long it takes. Amen.*

He's Paying Attention

As for me, I look to the LORD for help. I wait confidently for
God to save me, and my God will certainly hear me.
MICAH 7:7 NLT

"Mom." You say her name, but she's distracted, not really paying attention.

"Mom!" You say it a little louder, but she's still off in her own world, focused on something else.

"Mom!" You shout the word and she turns to you, shocked.

"Why are you yelling at me?" she asks.

Sound familiar? Many times in this life we have to repeat ourselves to be heard. And no doubt we've made our loved ones repeat themselves a time or two as well.

Aren't you glad God isn't like that? You don't have to say, "Lord. Lord! *Lord!*" He hears you the first time and responds.

God will certainly hear you, girl, in good times and bad. You can look to Him for help, knowing He's right there, ears wide open!

———➤

Thanks for always hearing me when I cry out, Jesus. I'm humbled by
the truth that You're always listening to my cries. Thank You! Amen.

Blessed and Highly Favored

Because of our faith, Christ has brought us into this place of
undeserved privilege where we now stand, and we confidently
and joyfully look forward to sharing God's glory.
ROMANS 5:2 NLT

Have you ever felt "blessed and highly favored"? As a child of the Most High God, you most certainly are blessed! And there's no doubt He has granted you special favor from time to time.

Think of those things in light of today's verse: Christ has brought you to a place of. . .what? *Undeserved privilege.*

Think of those two words. Undeserved privilege is when you're given something you most certainly don't deserve. Think of a kid who's been grounded but his dad lets him off the hook at the last minute so that he can go to the movies with his friends. That's undeserved privilege.

And that, sweet girl, is what Jesus gave you when He died for you on the cross. You didn't deserve salvation. You didn't deserve eternity with Him. In fact, your sin should have separated you from a holy God.

But. . .

What Jesus did on the cross changed everything. And now, blessed and highly favored, you stand before Him, confident in what He has done for you and oh, so grateful!

I don't know how to begin to thank You for this undeserved privilege
You've lavished on me, Lord. I'm blessed beyond measure! Amen.

Your Story

*But if we look forward to something we don't yet
have, we must wait patiently and confidently.*
ROMANS 8:25 NLT

A new movie is coming out and you're so excited! You've been waiting for ages, it seems. You read the book. You know the story. You're crazy about the actors in the movie. Now it just has to get here so you can enjoy it in person.

Waiting for something fun carries a certain excitement with it. Like prepping for a big vacation, for instance. Or getting ready for summer camp. Planning for a family cruise or a trip to the Grand Canyon. Sometimes getting ready is half the fun.

God wants you to anticipate all the good things He's bringing your way, even before you see them with your eyes. He has so many good things in store for you. Sure, there are obstacles in life, but they're part of the story He is writing for your life. Be patient as you wait to see how He weaves them into the bigger picture.

The life ahead of you is going to be amazing, girl! So face it confidently. Don't worry about tomorrow. Don't fret. Just look at your life as one epic upcoming movie that you haven't watched yet. (It's going to get great reviews!)

---

*I'm so glad I can have confidence about where You are leading me,
Lord. Thank You for this amazing life You've given me. Amen.*

Full to Overflowing

I pray that God, the source of hope, will fill you completely with joy and peace because you trust in him. Then you will overflow with confident hope through the power of the Holy Spirit.

ROMANS 15:13 NLT

What are you full of? Some people would say "hot air." Others might say "baloney." Some people might say, "She's full of herself." (Hopefully that's not the case!)

Look at today's verse. God wants you to be full of the things He is giving you—hope, joy, peace, and trust. All are good, positive things, straight from His heart to yours. When you allow those things to fill you up, you end up filled with something else: the power of the Holy Spirit.

In other words, God's gifts multiply! You don't just have hope. You don't just have trust. You don't just have joy and peace. . .you get the whole package!

When God fills you up, it's like a water glass full to the brim and running over. He's extremely generous with you, girl! He's not scrimping. No, He's lavishing His good gifts on you!

Be full to overflowing with His Spirit today. He wants this for you!

------------→

Thank You for filling me to overflowing, Jesus! You fill me completely, and I'm so grateful for Your gifts! Amen.

A Mountain of Priorities

*Then you will be able to live as the Lord wants and will always
do what pleases him. Your lives will produce all kinds of good
deeds, and you will grow in your knowledge of God.*
COLOSSIANS 1:10 GNT

Sometimes priorities can seem like a mountain looming in front of you. There are so many things you want out of this life, and they all seem like good things. Friends. Activities. Academics. Talents and abilities. Church community. Service opportunities. Strong family relationships.

All good, right? So how do you figure out how to prioritize without problems rising up like mountains in your path?

You know how it is: you want to do something with your friend on Saturday, but you've already committed to something else. Or maybe your parents ask you to help deep clean the house on Saturday, but you already told your friend you'd hang out.

All important things.

When all is said and done, you want to live a life that's pleasing to the Lord, right? It might seem hard, but when you prioritize and put the most important things first, He'll always make room for the other stuff that is meant to be.

Even if it means you don't always get to hang out with your friends.

$$\longrightarrow$$

*I want to do what pleases You, Lord. Show me how to
prioritize so that I can bless You and others. Amen.*

Where Is Your Treasure?

For where your treasure is, there will your heart be also.
LUKE 12:34 ESV

Imagine you're at school and you get an alert that a burglar is in your home. You pull up the camera app that your parents installed and watch the sneaky bad guy as he slips from room to room in your house.

Your heart is pounding harder than ever when he gets to your parents' room because you know your grandmother's wedding ring—the one she left to your mom—is in the jewelry box. Will the bad guy find it and take it?

This might seem like a silly illustration, but here's the point: You know where the treasure is. It's in your parents' room. So that's where your mind goes. That's where your thoughts go.

It's the same with anything you treasure. Your heart is linked to the treasure.

This is why Jesus wants you to treasure Him above all. May your thoughts always rush to Him—in good times and in bad.

———————

You are my treasure, Jesus! My thoughts are continually on You. May I always care more about You than anything else this world has to offer. Amen.

Two Masters

*"No one can serve two masters. Either you will hate the one
and love the other, or you will be devoted to the one and
despise the other. You cannot serve both God and money."*
MATTHEW 6:24 NIV

Imagine you've got a new job. Your boss is a lady named Maggie. Only, there's another boss, a man named Joe. Maggie tells you to do one thing; Joe tells you to do something else. Now you're confused. Who do you listen to? Who do you obey?

That's kind of how it is when you try to serve both God and money. They're two separate bosses. The drive to have more money will always be tugging at you, saying, "C'mon! Do what I say! Enjoy the high life!" And then there's God's voice, saying, "Trust Me, child. Don't set your sights on money. Set your sights on Me."

Money doesn't have to be a mountain, girl. But if you're always chasing after it, it will be.

Don't serve two masters. God is the only one you'll need. When you put your trust in Him, He'll make sure you have all the money you need.

---

*I trust You, Jesus. You're my only master! I won't make an idol
out of money. I won't chase after it, thinking it can take Your
place. I trust You to provide all that my family needs. Amen.*

Superheroes

No, in all these things we are more than
conquerors through him who loved us.
ROMANS 8:37 ESV

It's one thing to be a conqueror; it's another thing to be more than a conqueror.

Think of a war hero. Not your average war hero, but the guy who ran into the burning building to save a dozen children. He was wounded in the effort, but he wasn't concerned for his own safety. No, his eye was on the prize of saving others.

Now his bravery is being rewarded. He's being given a Purple Heart. Everyone knows he's a superhero.

You can be a spiritual superhero, girl. You can be the one running into the burning building to save others who are spiritually lost. There will be times when you care more about their salvation than your own reputation, and God will honor that. He's making you into a young woman of great valor, one He is uber-proud of!

Point me toward the ones who need to know You, Jesus.
I want to be the one who rushes in to make sure they have the
message of salvation. Thank You for making me more than a
conqueror, especially when it comes to those I love! Amen.

He's Got You Covered!

Keep your life free from love of money, and be content with what you have, for he has said, "I will never leave you nor forsake you."
HEBREWS 13:5 ESV

Why do you suppose the Bible merges these two seemingly different ideas—love of money and God's promise that He won't leave us? Interesting, right?

Here's the thing: when you don't really trust that God has your back, you'll fret over money. It's true. If you didn't believe He would really provide for you (as He promises in His Word), then you would probably try to fix every financial situation on your own, which means you would slave away, trying to make money.

He loves your work ethic, by the way, but there's no reason to panic over financial things. He's got you covered. No, really. He sees every need that you (or your parents) have. He's already making provision for those things. And even when you don't see the finances yet, remember. . .He sees into tomorrow and He's got it covered, girl.

I'm so glad You see into tomorrow, Jesus! I will be content with what I have, and I will trust You for everything I need. Amen.

The Mountain of Division

By the authority of our Lord Jesus Christ I appeal to all of you, my friends, to agree in what you say, so that there will be no divisions among you. Be completely united, with only one thought and one purpose.
1 CORINTHIANS 1:10 GNT

God hates division. He didn't create us to be divided into different camps. The church of Jesus Christ should be a growing, thriving entity, affecting the world for the better.

The problem is, we spend so much time fighting, backbiting, and disagreeing with one another that we're not always very productive for the kingdom. You see it all the time—in churches, between friends, and so on. People get irritated with their pastors. Or the style of music the church uses. Or the way people dress. Or the approach the church takes toward various traditions.

Things can get tricky because, as many people as you have in a congregation, that's how many opinions there will be. (Can you imagine the poor pastor trying to make everyone happy at once when they all have different ideas about how things should be done?)

Division is an especially large mountain, and every believer needs to work double-time to knock it down. Why? So that we can influence this world, of course. And also because the Lord is pleased when we walk in unity.

I will do my best to knock down the wall of division, Jesus! Amen.

Praise Knocks Down Mountains

Shout for joy to the LORD, all the earth. Worship the
LORD with gladness; come before him with joyful songs.
Know that the LORD is God. It is he who made us, and we
are his; we are his people, the sheep of his pasture.
PSALM 100:1–3 NIV

Wondering how to get through a really difficult time? Praise your way through. Struggling to figure out where you fit in with your peers? Praise your way through that too.

No matter what you're going through, no matter how high the mountains in front of you, you can literally praise your way through.

There's an amazing story in Acts 16 where Paul and Silas have been imprisoned for sharing the gospel. (And you thought you had it tough as a believer!) There they were in jail with a bunch of real criminals! Want to guess what they did? They starting singing and praising God.

Wondering what happened next? A massive earthquake hit and busted open the prison doors! (Clearly, not a coincidence! A *God*-incidence!)

We'll never know if their shouts of joy, their songs of praise, caused that earthquake. But we do know that they brought honor to God in the very depths of their pain, and He took care of them by setting them free.

He'll set you free too. So what are you waiting for? Sing, girl. Sing!

⟫———————→

I'll shout for joy even when I don't feel like it,
Jesus. Set me free through praise! Amen.

A Mountain of Sickness

God gave Paul the power to perform unusual miracles.
When handkerchiefs or aprons that had merely touched
his skin were placed on sick people, they were healed
of their diseases, and evil spirits were expelled.
ACTS 19:11–12 NLT

Consider this story from the book of Acts. Paul, Silas, and Timothy traveled around telling people about Jesus. In some of the towns they visited, people were receptive. In other towns, not so much.

One way God convinced many of the people to believe was by performing miracles through these disciples. They prayed for sick people, and the sick people got well.

You might read that and think, *Wow, that would be a cool gift to have. What if I prayed for sick people and they got well?*

What if, indeed! Two thousand years have come and gone since then, but we still serve the very same God. The Bible says He's the same yesterday, today, and forever. He healed people then, and He's still in the healing business today.

And, girl. . .He can use you. Take the time to pray. Stand in the gap for someone who's facing the mountain of sickness. Picture that wall tumbling to the ground as you stand and believe in prayer.

I'll keep believing for those who are hurting and sick, Lord
Jesus. Heal them according to Your will, I pray. Amen.

The Enemy Top Spot

"You have heard that it was said, 'Love your neighbor, and hate your enemy.' But I tell you this: Love your enemies, and pray for those who persecute you. In this way you show that you are children of your Father in heaven. He makes his sun rise on people whether they are good or evil. He lets rain fall on them whether they are just or unjust."
MATTHEW 5:43–45 GW

If someone asked you to make a list of your enemies, how long would that list be? Who would make the top spot? And the spots under that?

Hopefully your list wouldn't be terribly long, but here's an interesting way to look at it, regardless. Jesus says to love the people whose names are on the list, even that person who's at the very top.

Yeah, it's hard. It might seem impossible, actually. And this might sound crazy, but you have to love them exactly the same way you would love the person in the "most loved" spot.

That's the way God loves. Even when we're at our worst—even when we treat Him like an enemy instead of our Savior—He loves us as if we were the best friends He ever had. He died for us even before we knew Him. And He would do it all over again too.

Enemies don't have to be mountains. When you love them as Christ loves you, those mountains dissolve before your very eyes.

I get it, Jesus. I'll save myself a lot of trouble and heartache if I somehow figure out how to love those who aren't so nice to me. This seems impossible to me right now, but I know with You, all things are possible. Amen.

He Crafted You!

For we are his workmanship, created in Christ Jesus for good works,
which God prepared beforehand, that we should walk in them.
EPHESIANS 2:10 ESV

Imagine you've been given the task of creating a doll that walks, talks, and chews gum. You work for months to get her to work the way she should. Then, just about the time you're ready to present your doll to the world, she starts acting crazy! Instead of talking, she starts shouting. Instead of walking, she lies down and kicks her feet. Instead of chewing gum, she throws it at people.

This might seem like a crazy example, but God must feel like that doll maker sometimes! He created us to live a certain way. We do the opposite. He expects us to walk in a way that represents Him, and we throw a hissy fit instead. He calls us to speak His message and we jabber about anything but.

In short, we don't pay attention to the one who made us. We ignore the reason we were created, just like that doll choosing to throw her gum.

God made you with a purpose and for a purpose. Many of the mountains you face come as a result of ignoring His purposes for Your life. So follow the maker's instructions, girl! Things will go much easier for you if you do!

Thank You for creating me and calling me to this life,
Jesus. I know there's a purpose for my life. I don't want
to disappoint You or dishonor You in any way. Show me
how to glorify You in everything I do and say. Amen.

The Mountain of Social Media

*I appeal to you therefore, brothers, by the mercies of
God, to present your bodies as a living sacrifice, holy and
acceptable to God, which is your spiritual worship. Do not be
conformed to this world, but be transformed by the renewal
of your mind, that by testing you may discern what is the
will of God, what is good and acceptable and perfect.*
ROMANS 12:1–2 ESV

Are you addicted to social media? Are you one of those girls who's glued to her phone, waiting for the next post or private message from a friend?

Do you give too much time and attention to what other people are sharing? Let's face it—social media can be a huge distraction these days. And if you're not careful, it can become consuming. Before you realize it, you've spent hours a day "checking in" to see what's going on with others.

A little socialization is okay, but when it becomes a lifeline, things get problematic! Mountains rise up when the internet becomes your best friend. . .or your worst enemy.

Spend time with real people. Face-to-face time. Go to the park. Visit your neighbor. Hang out with that elderly woman down the street who wants to teach you to bake.

There's a time and place for social media, but "all the time" and "all over the place" isn't it! There are people right in front of you who are hungry for your time and attention, girl. Shower it on them!

*Lord, I don't want to get so wrapped up in social media
that I forget to spend time one-on-one with people.
Show me who I can visit today, I pray. Amen.*

How Are You Using Your Words?

Don't say anything that would hurt another person. Instead, speak only what is good so that you can give help wherever it is needed. That way, what you say will help those who hear you.
EPHESIANS 4:29 GW

Words can be used as weapons, or they can be used to bring healing. The choice is up to you.

Tonight before you go to bed, sit down with a piece of paper. Make a list of all the people you spoke to today. Then divide the page into two columns: one for positive, uplifting words and the other for negative, unthoughtful words.

Be honest! Write down the good and the bad. Rethink your conversations—with your parents, your siblings, your teachers, and your friends. Even that guy in the hallway at school who glared at you. And that girl. . .you know the one.

How did you use your words today? Were they used to bring life. . .or death? Were they poured out as an offering or aimed like weapons?

Words have so much power! Maybe that's why Jesus was intentional about telling us to use them wisely.

Speak only what is good. It won't be easy, but if you start focusing on it now, you'll do a better job tomorrow.

Show me how to guard my tongue, Lord Jesus! I cause so many problems with what I say. I make mountains where there shouldn't be any mountains! Teach me how to use my words for good, to bring life, I pray. Amen.

A Mountain of Gossip

At the same time, they learn to go around from house to house since they have nothing else to do. Not only this, but they also gossip and get involved in other people's business, saying things they shouldn't say.

1 Timothy 5:13 GW

Have you ever met someone who loved to gossip? These kinds of people are like the ones described in the verse above—they go from house to house (or class to class at school) getting in other people's business and saying things they shouldn't.

Why do you suppose humans are so hyperfocused on what other people do? Why do we think it's our business to judge others without realizing our own flaws?

Jesus wants you to spend more time analyzing your own heart and leaving your friends and fellow students to Him. He sees their flaws. And He sees yours too. And He's willing to love all of you, in spite of those flaws.

One last question: Has God ever gossiped about you? No? Then be like Him. Only speak words of affirmation and love, and you'll have a much smoother time!

I'm sorry for the times I've been a gossip, Lord. I don't know why it's so exciting and fun to focus on the flaws of others and talk about all the things they do wrong. Help me to guard my tongue. I really do want to be more like You, but I'm definitely going to need Your help! Amen.

Can't We All Get Along?

I, a prisoner in the Lord, encourage you to live the kind of life which proves that God has called you. Be humble and gentle in every way. Be patient with each other and lovingly accept each other. Through the peace that ties you together, do your best to maintain the unity that the Spirit gives.

EPHESIANS 4:1–3 GW

Getting along with others. It's not always easy, is it? And yet God encourages you to do your very best to live humbly with the people in your world. He wants you to treat them gently, like a mother with a child. God longs for you to be patient and understanding, lovingly accepting them.

So who are these people you're supposed to go out of your way for? They're all around you! And, girl. . .let's get real. It starts at home. Some of the biggest obstacles you'll face, relationship-wise, are inside the walls of your own home.

Talking back to your mom, ignoring your sister, rolling your eyes when your dad turns his back. . .none of these actions exhibit patience, loving acceptance, or unity. It's not always easy to love those we're closest to. Sometimes they're the hardest to get along with. But you'll have a much smoother life if you handle your relationships with family members the way God expects: loving them the way He does.

Be kind. Be gentle. Be patient.

Be like Him.

$$\text{\textgreater\textgreater\textgreater} \longrightarrow$$

Lord, I want to be more like You when it comes to the way I treat my family members and friends. Give me the patience I need to get along with them the way You want me to. Amen.

Take a Step Back

Welcome people who are weak in faith, but don't get into an argument over differences of opinion.
ROMANS 14:1 GW

Okay, this is a tough one. It's so hard not to argue, especially when you're sure that you're right. (And you usually feel that way, if you're like most people.)

Some people aren't as strong in their faith. Maybe they've only been serving Jesus for a short time. And they keep messing up. You want to fix them, but they don't seem to get it. They're not seeing or acknowledging the problem.

Take a step back, girl! God can reveal Himself to others. He doesn't want you to get in the way. Sure, there will be times when you'll need to rescue a friend, but don't make it a habit. And remember, new believers are on a learning curve. It takes time to grow strong in the faith. And even those who've been walking with the Lord for years still make mistakes. We don't always get it right.

So don't allow a misguided need to win every argument to taint your relationships. If you do, you'll create mountains that were never meant to be there.

>>>————————→

I don't want to add more mountains to my life, Jesus! I won't go around looking to pick a fight with people just because we disagree over something the Bible says or over the way we should be living. I'll trust You to fix the people I love. Amen.

Not Ashamed

For I am not ashamed of this Good News about Christ.
It is the power of God at work, saving everyone who
believes—the Jew first and also the Gentile.
ROMANS 1:16 NLT

Have you ever felt ashamed of yourself? Maybe you told yourself, *I'm not going to eat any chocolate chip cookies*, but then you ate four. Okay, five. Or maybe you told yourself, *I'm going to get up half an hour early every morning to read my Bible and pray*. Only, you didn't.

Maybe you're ashamed of your grades. Or the way you look. Maybe you carry the weight of shame over something you did years ago that you just can't seem to get over. Or maybe you're ashamed of your family—someone else's issues are causing you embarrassment.

There are a thousand reasons we might feel embarrassed or ashamed in this life, but here's one you should never give in to: don't be ashamed of the gospel. Don't be ashamed of your relationship with Jesus. Don't ever be embarrassed to call yourself a Christian, even in front of those who don't believe.

Hold your head up high and remember that the power of God is at work when you say, "I believe!" You can say to others, "Hey, if God saved me, He'll save anybody!" It's true, you know. He won't rest until all come to know who He is.

———————————→

I won't be ashamed of the gospel, Jesus. How could I be? It's the good news that saved my life and gave me the promise of eternity! Amen.

A New Song

He put a new song in my mouth, a song of praise to our God.
Many will see and fear, and put their trust in the LORD.
PSALM 40:3 ESV

Have you ever gotten hooked on a song you heard on the radio? Maybe you woke up singing it. Or maybe you were in the middle of doing the dishes and didn't even realize you were singing until your mom said, "You're singing that same song again."

It's hard to get a song out of your head once it's stuck, isn't it?

That's kind of how it is once you give your heart to Jesus. The more mountains He moves out of your life, the louder your song gets. And the louder your song gets, the more people notice the changes going on inside your heart.

Here's a challenge: Even on the bad days, go right on singing. When you're having a terrible, horrible, no-good, very bad day. . .let it rip! The enemy won't know what to do with you if you spend your lousy day worshipping the Creator. He'll have to turn and run in the opposite direction!

Many will see and put their trust in God. Wow! Did you realize your rejoicing has that kind of impact on your community? It does, girl. . .so keep on singing!

I won't let a bad day trip me up, Jesus! I'll go right on singing no matter how tough things get! I'm trusting You with all the rest. Amen.

Honestly?

"Never lie when you testify about your neighbor."
Exodus 20:16 GW

Do you know how many mountains rise up between friends because of dishonesty? A lot! Maybe a friend has a falling out with you. A third friend gets involved. Gossip takes place. Things are shared that shouldn't be.

Before long, stories get back to the first person. Then chaos breaks loose! Feelings are hurt and you find yourself saying things like, "Who, me? I never said anything like that!"

Only, you did. And then some. In fact, if your friend knew all the things you said, she'd probably never speak to you again.

Consider this verse from Exodus 20:16: "Never lie when you testify about your neighbor." You want to make sure that every story you share about others is the absolute truth—every word. No exaggeration. No slants. Just the facts, ma'am!

Things will simmer down with your friend if you put a cap on the gossip. And if you do feel the need to share with a trusted mentor or confidant, make sure it's for the purpose of prayer, so that your mentor can pray with you for God's intervention.

Friend issues really can quiet down with a little help from you!

I don't want to let gossip or lies come between me and my friends, Jesus. It's not always easy to keep my mouth closed. I need Your help with this one, Lord. Amen.

Lift Him Up!

*"And when I am lifted up from the earth,
I will draw everyone to myself."*
JOHN 12:32 NLT

What does it mean for Jesus to be lifted up?

Think about it this way: When you speak well of Him, when you share the exciting stories of what He's done in your heart, your life, and your family, you're lifting Him up.

When you tell a friend who's sick about that time God healed your grandmother, you're lifting Him up.

When you tell that girl in school who's struggling with peer pressure about the time you overcame in that area, you're lifting Him up.

When you're kind to your little brother or do the dishes the first time your mom asks, you're lifting Him up.

Your whole life can be a message to the world about Jesus. You can decide to lift Him up. . .or not. The choice is up to you. But think of what a difference you'll make if you make the right choice!

---

*Today I choose to be a message to the world about You, Jesus.
I will let others know who You are with my words, my actions,
and my testimony. I'll tell them about the mountains You've
helped me knock down. Give me courage, I pray! Amen.*

Those Icky Obstacles

Count it all joy, my brothers, when you meet trials of various kinds, for you know that the testing of your faith produces steadfastness. And let steadfastness have its full effect, that you may be perfect and complete, lacking in nothing.
JAMES 1:2–4 ESV

Have you ever kept a joy journal? Some people would call it a gratitude journal. Basically, you write down all of the things you're grateful for each day.

Sure, some days the list might seem smaller than other days, but resolving to write down the things you're thankful for can really put the troubles of the day in perspective. (Let's face it—the good almost always outweighs the bad when we pause to think about how blessed we are.) Looking over your list each day will help you learn to be grateful for all the things that work out!

Here's one thing you can be really grateful for: the trials you're facing right now are growing you into a girl who's going to be ever stronger in her faith. That's a good thing. In the end, you'll be a testimony to the goodness of God.

Count it all joy. . .even when you don't feel like it. You bring honor to Jesus when you look for (and find) the good.

I'm looking for the good, Jesus! I will count it all joy—the good, the bad, and the ugly. I'll look for the blessings even in the middle of the pain. Amen.

A Little While

*And after you have suffered a little while, the God of all
grace, who has called you to his eternal glory in Christ,
will himself restore, confirm, strengthen, and establish you.*
1 PETER 5:10 ESV

"Why do bad things happen to good people?"

Has anyone ever asked you this question? Maybe someone challenged your faith by saying, "If there was a God, He wouldn't let terrible things happen. Babies wouldn't die. Earthquakes wouldn't kill people. Storms wouldn't come."

Here's the truth, though it's a hard message to convey to unbelievers: we live in a fallen world. As a result, we'll experience suffering and pain. We're not in heaven yet. But even as we walk through the hardest of days, we have the peace of Christ to see us through. Today's verse really encapsulates His thoughts: after "a little while" God will restore, confirm, strengthen, and establish you.

He'll restore. That means He'll give back what the enemy has stolen. Even when your family has really been through it.

He'll confirm. He won't leave you wondering if He's there for you. You'll know it in your knower.

He'll strengthen you. And usually right when you need it most!

He'll establish you. He'll settle the issue in your heart and remind you of why you were put on this earth in the first place.

➤➤➤———————→

*Thank You that the suffering only lasts a little while, Jesus.
Even now, You're restoring, confirming, strengthening,
and establishing me. I'm so grateful! Amen.*

A Long-Distance Romance

You love him, although you have not seen him, and you believe in him, although you do not now see him. So you rejoice with a great and glorious joy which words cannot express, because you are receiving the salvation of your souls, which is the purpose of your faith in him.

1 PETER 1:8–9 GNT

Have you ever fallen in love with someone you haven't even met? Sounds kind of crazy, right? These days it happens all the time with Internet romances and other long-distance romances.

God has a long-distance romance that goes above and beyond anything you could experience here on earth: He loves you and woos you and cares for you beyond anything man could do. And He wants to be loved in return!

How do you love a God you haven't seen? Once you've given your heart to Him, take time every day to talk to Him. Spend serious one-on-one time with Him. Go for a walk and share—your heart, your joys, your sorrows, your trials. He wants to hear it all!

You'll overcome mountains if you stick close to the one who loves you most. And even though you can't see Him with your eyes, you have the joy of knowing He adores you, on good days and bad! While your relationship with the Lord may feel like a long-distance relationship, Jesus is closer than your next breath. He's right there, ready to share it all with you!

It's so great to know You love me, Jesus! And You're close by! I don't have to sign on to the internet to find You. I don't even have to pick up my phone. I just have to whisper Your name, and You're so close I could reach out and touch You! Thank You for loving me like that. Amen.

The Battlefield

What then shall we say to these things?
If God is for us, who can be against us?
ROMANS 8:31 ESV

Imagine you are a soldier headed to the battle. You go to the frontlines only to discover that no other warriors have come with you. Not even one. Across the battlefield you can see that the enemy has a huge group of people ready to take you down. He's not alone.

How would that make you feel? Doomed, right?

Here's the thing, though: there really will be times when it's just you and Jesus. No one else will be on the battlefield with you. And the enemy of your soul will be standing there with all his minions, taunting you, trying to convince you that you don't stand a chance.

Then you read a verse like the one above. If God is for you (and He is), then it doesn't matter how many people come against you. It's inconsequential. There could be a thousand warriors on the other side of the field and God would still take care of you.

It happened to David, the shepherd boy. He stared at that giant, Goliath, and probably should have been sweating! But instead, he understood and fully believed that God would come through for him. And He did! God proved Himself in a mighty way that day when the giant came tumbling down.

Your giants will fall too. God is for you.

I'm so grateful I don't have to worry about my enemies,
Jesus! Thanks for taking care of them for me! Amen.

They Won't Last Long, Girl

For our present troubles are small and won't last very long. Yet they produce for us a glory that vastly outweighs them and will last forever!
2 CORINTHIANS 4:17 NLT

Doesn't it bring great comfort to hear that your present troubles won't last very long? You might argue that they don't always feel small, but at least they're not going to last forever.

When you're in the middle of a crisis, though, your troubles can seem overwhelming. Satan is skilled at convincing you the problems will never go away. But one day you'll be able to put things in perspective, to look back and say, "Wow, I remember when that happened!" and realize the pain of it is no longer so fresh.

Let's do a little experiment. Think back on something bad that happened a year ago. Or maybe two years ago. Or ten. Remember how horrible it was in the moment? Remember how it broke your heart and brought you so much grief?

Are you still feeling it the way you were then? No, because you've had the blessing of time.

Some people would say that time heals all wounds. The truth is, God heals all wounds. . .but He uses time to do it.

>>>———————>

Thank You for the blessing of time, Jesus. I'm so glad my troubles won't last forever. These mountains will disappear and be a thing of the past! Amen.

Grow Up!

*Don't let anyone look down on you because you are
young, but set an example for the believers in speech,
in conduct, in love, in faith and in purity.*
1 TIMOTHY 4:12 NIV

Yes, you're younger than the adults in your world. And yes, there will be times some adults think you need to wise up or act more maturely. (They may be right!)

Here are some ways to set an example for others so that no one ever questions your maturity level: First, watch what you say. Don't knee-jerk or be a reactor. Your mouth will give you away every time (and will cause mountains to rise up unnecessarily).

Second, it's not just your mouth; it's your actions. People are watching. Some are watching closely. You represent Jesus, girl! Act like it!

Third, love others. In fact, God wants you to love them the way you love yourself and to treat them accordingly.

Fourth, be a person of faith! Believe. . .even when things seem impossible. Again, people are watching! When they see mountains falling in your life, they will know you're a woman of faith!

Finally, guard your purity—this shows up in your actions, your interactions with the opposite sex, the way you dress, the people you hang out with, even the places you go.

If you do all these things, no one will ever have reason to look down on you because you are young!

$$\longmapsto\!\!\!\!\!\longrightarrow$$

*Lord, help me to guard what I say, how I live, and who I hang out with.
I know others are watching, and I want to represent You well! Amen.*

Your Hideaway

For he will conceal me there when troubles come; he will hide me in his sanctuary. He will place me out of reach on a high rock.
<small>PSALM 27:5</small> <small>NLT</small>

Have you ever watched a lizard run along the edge of a fence? His body is an interesting shade of brown. Then he jumps into a tree and runs across the leaves. His body miraculously transforms into a lovely shade of green.

Lizards have the uncanny ability to blend in so that they're not noticed by predators. And that's exactly what God is promising you in the verse above. He's concealing (hiding) you away when troubles come. You're like that little lizard, escaping the predator. God places you on a high rock and makes you invisible to the enemy, which gives you a chance to catch your breath!

Aren't you glad you serve a God who sees and knows when trouble is coming? He cares about you deeply and wants to remind you that He's got you covered no matter what mountains you're facing.

———»»»————→

You're such an awesome protector, Lord God! Thanks for looking out for me and giving me strategies to outwit the enemy! You've made me invisible to him! Amen.

She's Innocent!

Answer me when I call to you, O God who declares me innocent.
Free me from my troubles. Have mercy on me and hear my prayer.
PSALM 4:1 NLT

God declares you innocent. Maybe you don't feel innocent. Maybe you just finished pitching a major fit in front of your mom and now you feel awful. You upset her. You even made her cry. You went back and apologized, but you can't forgive yourself.

Then you read a scripture like this. God says you're innocent?

Here's the truth, girl: When God looks at you, it's through a veil. He sees you through the work of His Son, Jesus, on the cross. When Jesus died for you, He washed you whiter than snow. This doesn't mean you won't make mistakes. You will. But your forgiveness has been bought and paid for on the cross.

There are twelve words that will heal any relationship, and these words will knock over the mountain of guilt you're feeling too. Are you ready? Here they are: "I am sorry. I was wrong. Please forgive me. I love you." Speak those twelve words to the people in your life who need to hear them and then watch as God mends the broken places, even the feelings of guilt and shame in your heart.

Thank You for the reminder that I'm already forgiven,
Jesus! I'm so grateful Your sacrifice on the cross washed
away my sins once and for all. Thank You too for knocking
down the mountain of guilt that I have faced. Amen.

A Ring of Troubles

*Though I am surrounded by troubles, you will protect
me from the anger of my enemies. You reach out your
hand, and the power of your right hand saves me.*
PSALM 138:7 NLT

Have you ever played Duck-Duck-Goose? You know how everyone is seated in a circle? Now imagine you're trapped on the inside of that circle with no way out. They're a bunch of ducks and you're a goose!

Sometimes life feels like that. You feel like you're trapped inside a ring of troubles. They're all ganging up on you, chasing you down! And there doesn't seem to be a way to penetrate the wall of trouble to get to the other side.

Take a look at today's verse. God promises to protect you even when you're totally surrounded by troubles. Those enemies who are staring you down? Those mountains that are looming in a big circle around you? They're nothing when compared to the mighty hand of God!

With one fingertip, He can knock those troubles down! His hand can save you no matter how trapped you're feeling. And remember, when you're walking in the fullness of a relationship with Jesus, you're never really trapped. He's always right there, ready to fight on your behalf.

---

*Thank You, Jesus, for always protecting me. No matter how
trapped I feel, You're right there, ready to deliver me. Amen.*

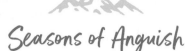

Seasons of Anguish

I will be glad and rejoice in your unfailing love, for you have seen my troubles, and you care about the anguish of my soul.
PSALM 31:7 NLT

What do you think of when you read the word *anguish*? Anguish is a deep, twisting kind of pain. Think of how you wring out a dishcloth after using it. The pressure you use to squeeze out the water is the same kind of crushing pressure that anguish can cause.

People in anguish are doubled over. They can't see the road out in front of them. They're too focused on the ground below.

Seasons of anguish will come. And honestly? Those mountains in front of you may seem so insurmountable that you absolutely refuse to look at them. They tower over you like impossible obstacles.

So you keep your focus on the ground and pray it doesn't swallow you up.

Now think all of that in light of today's verse. God has seen your troubles. He cares about the anguish of your soul. Your response is to stand upright, face the mountain, and begin to praise Him, even before you see it cast into the sea. You truly can rejoice in His unfailing love and be glad. . . even when you haven't seen your miracle yet. Now that's faith!

→

I'll do my best to rejoice and be glad even when the situation has yet to change, Lord Jesus. Give me Your eyes to see those mountains moved! Amen.

Fully Engaged

Please listen and answer me,
for I am overwhelmed by my troubles.
PSALM 55:2 NLT

Have you ever received a spam call from someone trying to sell you something? Maybe you rolled your eyes as they dove into their message, which they hoped would win you over. They were talking, but you weren't really listening.

Or maybe your kid sister starts telling you a random story from her day; you're not really interested, but you act like you are. (These things happen.)

Aren't you glad God isn't like that? He's fully engaged when you share something with Him. If you come to Him with your troubles (and He really hopes you will), then He's right there, leaning in close to hear not just your words, but your heart.

How cool would it be if you listened to others the way God listens to you? Would it change your relationships? Would the mountains your friends and family members are facing seem smaller to them if you showed that you truly cared?

It's so easy to listen. Just lean in close, like Jesus does.

I'm leaning in close to You today, Jesus, so that I can
hear Your heartbeat. Teach me to love like You love and
care like You care. I want to help my loved ones face their
mountains so they know they're not alone. Amen.

The Stupidity of a Short Temper

A person of great understanding is patient,
but a short temper is the height of stupidity.
PROVERBS 14:29 GW

Have you ever known anyone with a short fuse? Maybe he blows up at every little thing. He's red in the face. His hands are clenched. He raises his voice. Ugh. Those people are tough to be around.

Most people would just say, "He's got a temper," but God would say, "That short temper of his is the height of stupidity."

Why is a short temper stupid? Well, think about it. People who don't take the time to be understanding don't hold on to relationships very long, do they? They end up turning people against them. They create enemies unnecessarily. Then they wonder why they have so many mountains in their lives. Most are brought on by their own carelessness.

Don't be one of those people. Don't let your anger become a mountain in your life. Speak to it now, while you're young. When you start to feel that temper mounting, walk away. Take a deep breath. Count to ten. Ask for God's help. He wants to help you get past this now, before it becomes a habit.

I don't want to have a short temper, Jesus! Please guard my heart.
Guard my tongue. Help me not to blow up at every little thing.
May the mountain of anger be gone from my life. . .forever! Amen.

A Dead-End Road

Stop being angry! Turn from your rage!
Do not lose your temper—it only leads to harm.
PSALM 37:8 NLT

Have you ever accidentally turned onto a dead-end road? You can only go so far before you come screeching to a halt. The road ends. If you keep going, there will be an accident. A big one. Maybe you'll drive off the edge of a cliff. Maybe you'll end up in the river. Maybe you'll crash into a tree.

Those DEAD END signs are there for a reason! Those are roads not worth traveling.

Anger is a dead-end road. It leads to Nowheresville. When you get on that road, you crash and burn every time!

The problem is, once you're on that road it's hard to hit the brakes! You just want to keep going and going and going. But when you do, it never ends well.

So pay attention to today's verse. Turn away from that crazy dead-end street. Go a different way. You're going to wind up in a ditch if you don't turn things around.

Lord, I get it. My anger is getting me nowhere. . .except
in trouble! Help me tap the brakes. I want to stop this
rage before it gets me in an accident! Amen.

Don't React!

A soft answer turns away wrath, but a harsh word stirs up anger.
PROVERBS 15:1 ESV

When someone blows up at you, you have two choices: react. . .or act.

What's the difference? A person who "reacts" kicks back hard and fast, without taking the time to think the reaction through.

But a person who "acts" is careful. Methodical. Thoughtful. She's not knee-jerking. She's working a plan.

When you're faced with a tough individual, you need a plan. Always allowing yourself to kick back isn't a long-term strategy. You need a bona fide plan of action to turn away that person's wrath. If you simply respond in anger, the situation is just going to blow up on you like a bonfire out of control.

Put out the fire when it's small. Don't throw gasoline on it. Harsh words can lead to forest fires, after all.

---

*I see Your point, Jesus. Anger is like a mountain in my
life when I don't give soft answers. It's not always easy
to respond thoughtfully, especially with some people.
Teach me to be an "actor," not a "reactor," I pray. Amen.*

Get over It!

*"In your anger do not sin": Do not let the sun
go down while you are still angry.*
EPHESIANS 4:26 NIV

"Don't go to bed mad." Maybe you've heard that expression before. Some people would add, "Stay up and fight all night!"

Why do you think God cares so much about us wrapping up our arguments before dropping into bed at night?

Maybe it has something to do with the fact that each day has enough trouble of its own. When we go to bed mad, we wake up with unresolved issues with the person we're mad it. Basically, we're inviting anger to linger for an extra day.

Anger is a naughty guest. He needs to go as quickly as possible. Boot him out the door by putting an end to your arguments before you drop into bed. Then you can sleep peacefully. You won't stay up all night fretting over what you want to say to the person the next day. Everything is already spoken when you get it out before bedtime.

Troubles will come. Tempers will flare. But that naughty guest can't stay for long or your house won't be livable!

*I'll get over it, Jesus! I won't hang on to my anger or go to
bed knotted up in frustration! Show me how to end each day
totally at peace—with myself, others, and You. Amen.*

What's on Your Name Tag?

Control your temper, for anger labels you a fool.
ECCLESIASTES 7:9 NLT

Have you ever been to a conference or event where everyone had to wear a name tag? It helps to be able to see the name, doesn't it?

Now imagine you're at an event and someone hands you a name tag. But instead of your name, the tag reads, FOOL.

Um, what?

You try to pull it off, but it's stuck. Now what?

Now picture yourself remaining at the event with that label visible to everyone in attendance. They're laughing behind your back. And you don't blame them. They've all formulated an opinion of you.

That's kind of what it's like when you've behaved foolishly and created a reputation for yourself. It's hard to shake. People go on thinking poorly of you even after you prove them wrong. Reputations are a tough thing to fix.

Control your temper, girl. Don't give those people anything more to talk about!

I won't let the word Fool be on my name tag, Jesus. Thank You for helping me control the mountain of anger! Amen.

Keep It in the Pipes

Fools vent their anger, but the wise quietly hold it back.
PROVERBS 29:11 NLT

What does it mean to "vent" your anger? What is a vent, anyway?

Think about the air conditioner in your house. What good would it be for that cold air to sit in pipes in your attic or walls? It's only beneficial when it comes pouring out of the vents in the wall or ceiling, filling the room with chilly air. Aah! That's nice!

Anger needs to stay in the pipes. When you open the vents, it covers everything (and everyone) in the room. Even people you didn't mean to hurt.

Take a look at the verse above. What do wise people do? They quietly hold back their anger. They don't spew. They don't lose their cool. They keep their temper tamped down (in the pipes).

Why do you suppose God cares so much about this? He wants you to exhibit self-control so that you can be a lovely reflection of Him. Isn't that what He does when you mess up? Has there ever been one time when Jesus screamed at you or lashed out in anger at you? No way!

Don't let anger become a driving force in your life. Close the vent. Be like Jesus.

———————→

*I'm closing the vent today, Jesus! I've let my temper
cause too much trouble already. I won't heat up the room
with my frustrations. I want to be like You! Amen.*

What a List!

Also get rid of your anger, hot tempers, hatred,
cursing, obscene language, and all similar sins.
Colossians 3:8 gw

Whew! That's a long list of things God is asking you to get rid of, isn't it? Notice it all starts with one very important word: *anger.* If you can just get rid of anger, the rest of those things can disappear as well!

Maybe we'd better take a closer look at anger. Where does it come from, anyway, and how can you get rid of it? You don't consider yourself an angry person, after all. And yet. . .you occasionally have temper tantrums. And yes, you've been known to spout off a time or two. Or twelve. You've even used those three awful words: "I hate her!" or "I hate him!" a few times. So, clearly, anger is bubbling underneath the surface.

Let's break it down. You get frustrated. You're not really mad. . .at first. But then your frustration builds over time. Before long, you're like a teakettle boiling over. It started as a teensy-tiny thing that you didn't address. But once it started to build, it was like a package of canned biscuits about to pop. (Whoops—explosion! What a mess!)

Deal with the little frustrations when they come so that they don't become huge mountains, girl!

Lord, I have some little frustrations I need to bring to You
today. I'm going to start with _____. Amen.

Watch Your Words

"But I say, if you are even angry with someone, you are subject to judgment! If you call someone an idiot, you are in danger of being brought before the court. And if you curse someone, you are in danger of the fires of hell."
MATTHEW 5:22 NLT

Do you do a lot of name-calling? Ever flipped out on someone and called them an ugly name or two? It happens.

Have you ever considered the fact that name-calling breaks God's heart? He's not a fan. So before you lose it on your little sister or that kid in math class, stop and take a deep breath.

This name-calling thing might be a mountain in your life that you need to conquer. If you find yourself frequently losing your temper and resorting to words like *idiot* or *stupid*, then you might need to examine your heart.

People are motivated by kind words, not ugly ones. You know it's true. Has Jesus ever once called you an idiot? (How would you feel if He did?) He doesn't. . .because He adores you. He wants to encourage you to be the best you that you can be.

You can encourage that kid sister—or that boy in math class—by speaking positive, uplifting words in front of them. Even when you're mad. (*Especially* when you're mad.)

Your words have impact. Speak the ones that bring life, girl! Everyone will be glad you did.

Help me guard my tongue, Jesus. I don't want to break Your heart! I don't want to hurt others with my name-calling. Stop me before I do more damage, I pray. Amen.

My Way or the Highway

Love is patient and kind; love does not envy or boast; it is not arrogant
or rude. It does not insist on its own way; it is not irritable or resentful.
1 CORINTHIANS 13:4–5 ESV

Are you the kind of person who always wants to have her own way? Do you put your needs above the needs of others? If so, then living this way can feel like walking around with pebbles in your shoes. You'll never be completely happy or comfortable because—let's face it—things don't always go our way.

Instead of putting yourself first, God wants you to consider the needs of others to be as important as your own. That's not easy, is it? And it certainly doesn't come naturally. The Lord longs for you to be as patient with other people as you are with yourself. And (here's a hard one) He's also not a fan of people singing their own praises. (We've all done it.)

Now look at the part of the verse that addresses arrogance. If you've ever known someone who's stuck up, you can see why God threw that in. Arrogance is the great divider. When you're arrogant, you're always trying to prove you're better than others. God is definitely not a fan of that behavior.

Don't be prideful. Don't be rude. And don't insist on putting yourself first, girl.

Love others as you love yourself. That's God's way!

→

I'll get rid of the pebbles in my shoes when I start loving others with
the kind of patience You expect, Jesus. But I'll need Your help! Amen.

Leave It to Him

Don't take revenge, dear friends. Instead, let God's anger take care of it. After all, Scripture says, "I alone have the right to take revenge. I will pay back, says the Lord."
ROMANS 12:19 GW

"I alone." Why do you think God said it that way? Why did He take the time to say, "Let Me be the one to take revenge, not you"?

Chances are pretty good you've wanted to take revenge a time or two. Maybe you actually did, and it caused even more grief.

Mountains don't disappear when you take revenge, you know. They just get bigger than ever before! And if you take revenge against someone who has an army on his side, you'll soon be looking at a whole mountain range!

God gets angry too. And here's the thing: He's already planning to take care of things. He sees the injustice. He sees the ones who wronged you. And He's going to deal with it in His own time and His own way. If you jump in there and try to get even, you'll just get in God's way. And let's be honest: Wouldn't you prefer that He deal with the person anyway?

Leave it to Him.

I'll leave it to You and You alone, God! I won't try to get revenge. You'll do a much better job of dealing with the one who hurt me anyway. I trust that You will take care of things in Your own time and Your own way. Amen.

Girl Stuff

Your beauty should not come from outward adornment, such as
elaborate hairstyles and the wearing of gold jewelry or fine clothes.
Rather, it should be that of your inner self, the unfading beauty of
a gentle and quiet spirit, which is of great worth in God's sight.
1 PETER 3:3-4 NIV

Let's face it—we all want to look good. But sometimes this whole "keeping up with the girls" thing is tough. The clothes. The hair. The makeup. The jewelry. The nails. The shoes.

Ugh. It's a lot. Maybe you look at all of that as one giant obstacle. It's a mountain you don't want to climb. You'd rather just be you, and not follow the trends.

Good for you, girl! Don't get caught in the trap of feeling like you have to fit in—to look a certain way or wear your hair a certain way. You were never meant to be a clone of someone else.

When you read about all the great women in the Bible, you'll notice a common theme: the stories aren't usually focused on the woman's outward beauty but rather on the great things she accomplished for God. Or the obstacles she overcame. Take Hannah, for instance. Or Esther. (Sure, Esther was beautiful, but that isn't the point of the story! She was courageous! Her people were spared because of her bravery in facing the king on their behalf!)

Be like the great women in the Bible. Spend more time focusing on inner beauty than outer beauty and you'll accomplish great things!

→

Help me work on my inside beauty, Lord Jesus! Amen.

What Are You Wearing Today?

Strength and dignity are her clothing,
and she laughs at the time to come.
PROVERBS 31:25 ESV

There are some Bible verses, like the one above, that are puzzling, to say the least. The woman in this Bible story is dressed in strength and dignity? They're her clothes? (Does she sew them together with a needle and thread? How does that work, exactly?)

Let's unpack this verse to see if we can figure it out. Think of it this way: You have become "known" for a certain look. Maybe you love jeans and hoodies. Or maybe hats are your thing. Maybe you're into bright colors, or maybe you're one of those girls who wears mostly black or gray. Whatever it is, you've kind of become known for your look, whether you meant to or not.

The woman in this story has become known for her look. She's strong. She's dignified—she carries herself well and represents Jesus well. When people see her coming, they recognize her. . .and they recognize Jesus inside her!

Wear Him well, sweet girl. Be so close to Jesus that you reflect Him on good days and bad. He will dress you in His strength. That's a great look on anyone!

I am strong in You, Jesus. . .and I hope it shows! I want people
to see You when they look at me. So please dress me in Your
strength. Give me wisdom, kindness, and all Your traits.

Wonderfully Made

*I praise you because I am fearfully and wonderfully made;
your works are wonderful, I know that full well.*
PSALM 139:14 NIV

You are created in the image of a perfect Creator. Wow. Think about that! He took great care to craft you. Picture a toymaker in a shop, designing a doll. He works long and hard on her, choosing the eye color, hair color, facial expression, and so on. Now think of how much more time God invested in you!

He didn't miss a thing! Your smile. Your freckles. Your goofy laugh. Your personality. The wardrobe you prefer. The way you decorate your room. The way you interact with your friends. All of it. You had a master designer who thought of everything, right down to the last detail.

If He cares that much, He also must care about the troubles you face. When He designed you, He placed inside of you the power you would need to speak to the mountains that rise up in front of you.

$$\longrightarrow$$

I am wonderfully made! You didn't leave out a thing, Father God! I need to stop cutting myself down, I guess. If I'm really specially designed by You (and I know You don't make mistakes), then I have to learn to appreciate the person You've made me to be. Help me, I pray! Amen.

Finish Well

And I am certain that God, who began the good work
within you, will continue his work until it is finally
finished on the day when Christ Jesus returns.
PHILIPPIANS 1:6 NLT

Here's a question (and answer honestly, please): Do you always finish what you start? Maybe you start a project for school but fizzle out. Then just before it's due you go into a panic and throw together something you're not really proud of.

Or maybe you start a Bible reading plan but don't make it very far before giving up.

Hey, we all do it. Humans are, for the most part, great starters. . .but not great finishers.

God wants you to be a girl who finishes well. Run the race. . .all the way to the finish line. Even if you don't feel like it. (Especially if you don't feel like it.)

Take a look at today's verse. If God began a good work in you (and He did!), He's going to finish it. We serve a Savior who always finishes what He starts. If He started it, He will finish it. God is not a quitter.

You? You often give up when things get hard. Aren't you glad God isn't like that? He keeps going. . .and going. . .and going.

Don't believe it? Didn't He go all the way to the cross for you? Learn from His example! You'll conquer far more mountains if you don't give up, girl!

Help me to keep going even when I don't feel like it, Lord Jesus.
You started a good work in me. And You're going to finish it. Amen.

He Can Do It!

"For nothing will be impossible with God."
LUKE 1:37 ESV

Have you ever wondered what it would be like to have superhuman strength or to be able to do things that are seemingly impossible? (Fly like a bird, for instance. Or climb the highest mountain.)

If someone gave you the task of writing down all of the things that are impossible for you—a lone human being—to accomplish, it would be an incredibly long list. You can't create life. You can't heal diseases. You can't put broken relationships back together.

But God can. All the things that are impossible for you are totally doable for Him. In fact, He can accomplish those things in the blink of an eye, with just a word.

So what makes you think He can't tackle the problems you're facing? They're nothing to Him. (Literally. . .nothing.) Sure, they're huge obstacles to you, but that's because you're human. He's the Creator of all.

He can move your mountains. And He wants you to develop the faith to speak to them, totally believing that He can. . .and He will.

Thank You for the reminder that nothing is impossible with You, Jesus. All the things I can't do. . .You can! Increase my faith so that I can believe for the big stuff, I pray. Amen.

Take a Hike, Devil!

There isn't any temptation that you have experienced which is unusual for humans. God, who faithfully keeps his promises, will not allow you to be tempted beyond your power to resist. But when you are tempted, he will also give you the ability to endure the temptation as your way of escape.

1 CORINTHIANS 10:13 GW

"Why does the devil keep messing with me?" Maybe you've used those words. Maybe you've felt that way!

Here's a sobering truth: every believer is a target for the enemy. He wants to take down anyone who's doing anything good for God. And he won't stop until he's done his best to discourage you.

Girl, take heart! If you feel like you're being beaten up by the enemy, it's because he sees you as a warrior for God. He sees you as a threat, in other words! So look that enemy in the eye. Tell him to take a hike.

And remember, you're not alone. Believers all over the globe are facing the same troubles and temptations you are. But God won't let these things defeat you. He's going to give you the ability to endure and overcome them. And best of all, He's already plotting your escape from the enemy's trap!

God will show you how to get past this. He will. So hang on and don't give up!

I feel like I'm stuck in an escape room sometimes, Jesus. I'm totally overwhelmed and lost, and the enemy is after me hard and fast! Thank You for the reminder that I'll be able to get past this with Your help. Amen.

Altogether Beautiful

You are altogether beautiful, my darling, beautiful in every way.
SONG OF SOLOMON 4:7 NLT

Did you blush when you read today's scripture? Can you picture a guy saying those words to you? (Hey, let's face it—most guys aren't that good with words. They wouldn't put it quite like that.)

The Lord thinks you're perfect. Let that sink in. He thinks you're gorgeous inside and out. He uses words like *lovely, beautiful, darling,* and so on. (Who talks like that? Oh, right. The Lord!)

You're part of the church, the bride of Christ, lovely and pure. He's your groom, committed to you for all eternity.

Is all this marriage talk freaking you out? Don't let it! That's really the picture Jesus wants to plant in your brain. He wants you to feel as loved and protected as a new bride.

If He really sees you as being that special, then you have nothing to worry about. No troubles that pop up, no mountains that rise up, are too much for the bridegroom! He's got this. He'll protect you fiercely, at any cost. So relax, girl. And remember, when you look in the mirror, it's good to see yourself the way the Lord sees you.

You really are beautiful, you know.

Yes, you are.

$$\gg\!\!\!\gg \longrightarrow$$

This is a hard one for me, Lord Jesus! I don't always see myself as being beautiful or lovable. I'm kind of blown away that You feel this way about me. Help me to see myself the way You see me. (And by the way, thanks for being such a great protector!) Amen.

A Proud Papa

The Lord will hold you in his hand for all to see—
a splendid crown in the hand of God.
ISAIAH 62:3 NLT

Remember that scene in *The Lion King* where Simba's father, the king, holds him up to show him off to all the kingdom? Talk about a proud papa!

That's kind of what this verse brings to mind. God will hold you in His hand for all to see—a splendid crown in His hand.

Let's break that down. What does a king's crown represent? His authority. His position. It's also a symbol of wealth. Not just a symbol, really. The crown is literally loaded with jewels, items of immense value.

When God holds you, He's holding a priceless treasure. You carry His image, His passion, His love. You are His beloved child, the one He cherishes.

With all that in mind, why do you ever doubt Him? If He cares enough to show you off to the world, surely He can take care of a few mountains in your path! He holds you in the palm of His hand, girl!

———

Thank You for holding on to me and cherishing me,
Jesus! I'm so glad to be Your child! Amen.

Just Ask!

If any of you lacks wisdom, you should ask God, who gives
generously to all without finding fault, and it will be given to you.
JAMES 1:5 NIV

Have you ever read James 4:2, which basically says, "You have not because you ask not"? Well, that's definitely true when it comes to wisdom. Maybe you feel like you're short on wisdom. You keep making mistakes. You keep circling the same mountain time and time again. You wonder if you'll ever make it past this one problem spot.

Ask God to give you wisdom. He will, you know! He promises in the verse above that He will pour it out generously. (Hey, a parent who gives generously to his child goes above and beyond expectations!)

God will give you wisdom to get past this obstacle you're facing. Just ask Him and expect Him to move! He has never let you down before, and He doesn't plan to start now!

Lord, I need Your wisdom! I've tried in my own strength to
conquer this problem, but I just can't seem to. It's going to
take something bigger than me! My hands are open to receive.
Please pour out Your wisdom today, I pray! Amen.

He Sees. . .and He Cares

"Look at the birds of the air: they neither sow nor reap
nor gather into barns, and yet your heavenly Father
feeds them. Are you not of more value than they?"
MATTHEW 6:26 ESV

"God doesn't see me. He doesn't care. If He did, He would do something about this mess I'm in." You've probably said something like that. Or maybe you felt it but didn't say the words out loud.

Here's the truth: God sees and He does care. We live in a broken, fallen world, so things don't always work out the way we want, when we want. But it's not like God isn't paying attention. He is. And He Himself is heartbroken over much of what He sees.

Think about this: He created all of nature. He knows every bird flying in the sky right now. He knows every dog, every cat, every fish in the sea. Nothing gets by Him. Not one thing is unnoticed.

If He sees all His creation, He surely sees you. And He takes care of the needs of the birds. And the dogs and cats. And the fish. And everything else. If He gives them what they need, He'll make sure you have everything you need to knock down the mountains in front of you.

Don't give up. He sees you.

→→→

You're going to take care of me, Jesus. I'm sorry for the times I don't
trust You. I know You can see what I'm going through and You care.
Give me the courage I need to get through this, I pray! Amen.

Faith Is Key

"And whatever you ask in prayer, you will receive, if you have faith."
MATTHEW 21:22 ESV

We often say, "It's all up to God!" And it is. He's capable of anything. God is in the miracle-working business, after all. But often we have a role to play too.

Take a look at today's verse. The Lord tells us that we will receive whatever we ask for in prayer. . .if we have faith. It's not always easy, is it?

Let's say you're struggling through a tough season because your grand-mother is very ill. You wonder if she's going to pull through. You pray, but you really doubt God will choose to heal her.

Adding doubt to the mix doesn't help, girl! God wants you to increase your faith and to pray believing that He not only can but will! Whether He answers your prayer by healing her here on earth or by providing her with the ultimate healing (eternity with Him), you will have done your part by praying in total faith.

Don't stop believing, even when it's really, really hard. God will honor your faith if you stand strong and believe even when the circumstances look bleak.

→

*Please increase my faith, Lord Jesus! I want to have the
kind of faith that can believe for miracles! Amen.*

If You Really Believe Me. . .

And without faith it is impossible to please him,
for whoever would draw near to God must believe that
he exists and that he rewards those who seek him.
HEBREWS 11:6 ESV

Do you ever picture God looking down at you and saying, "Girl, you say you have all this faith, but I don't really see you acting on it! If you believe Me, act like it!"?

How do you prove your faith? When the going gets tough, don't panic! Keep speaking in faith. Draw near to Him. Don't pull away. Don't doubt His Word or His promises to you. He's a fulfiller of promises, and He won't let you go.

So when things get really hard, don't start weeping and wailing. Don't run for the hills or start saying a bunch of negative things out of fear. Instead, turn your heart toward Him and trust that He's got everything under control. He hasn't fallen off His throne, you know! He's going to stay there throughout eternity!

Please make my faith stronger, Jesus! Show me how to stay
courageous when the circumstances don't look good. I don't want
to panic or run the other way. I want to stick close to You! Amen.

Hear. . .and Learn

So faith comes from hearing,
and hearing through the word of Christ.
ROMANS 10:17 ESV

Faith comes by hearing.

That's true of a lot of things, isn't it? You don't know until someone tells you. How does a child learn to walk? He hears his mother say, "Come to Mommy!" while she extends her arms.

How did you learn to be courageous? By listening to people say, "You've got this!"

How did you learn algebra? By listening to your teacher as she wrote out the problems on the board.

You hear. . .you learn. And the lesson you're learning right now is a faith lesson. So listen to God's still, small voice. When He says, "We've got this, you and Me," He means it. And remember, you can listen to His Word too. It's loaded with verses that will activate your faith and cause you to grow.

The Lord is always talking.

Are you always listening? Probably not, but you can lean in close today!

$\longrightarrow$

I get it, Jesus! You want to grow my faith, but it's up
to me to keep my listening ears open. Please help
me do my best to hear Your voice. Amen.

Are You Absolutely, Positively Sure?

Now faith is the assurance of things hoped for,
the conviction of things not seen.
HEBREWS 11:1 ESV

"Are you sure?" a friend asks you. "Are you absolutely, positively, without a doubt sure?"

Suddenly, as he asks that question, you're not. You were a couple of minutes ago, but the question has planted doubt in your mind.

To be sure means you're confident in what you believe or know. You're not like a wave tossed around on the sea. You have supernatural confidence.

Take a look at today's Bible verse. To have faith means to be sure. You're absolutely, positively sure. . .of something that hasn't even happened yet! You're like a kid waiting for Christmas morning. You believe with everything inside of you that it's coming and that it's going to be awesome. You can't see it yet, but in your imagination it's very, very real.

That's how faith works. It looks at a tough situation and sees a better outcome. It sees through the lens of hope.

Increase my faith so I can be absolutely, positively sure,
Lord Jesus! I don't want to doubt. I want my faith to
blossom and grow. I don't know where You're taking
me, but I know it's going to be awesome! Amen.

Only God Can Do What Only God Can Do

For by grace you have been saved through faith.
And this is not your own doing; it is the gift of God,
not a result of works, so that no one may boast.
EPHESIANS 2:8–9 ESV

Aren't you glad it's not up to you? I mean. . .really! If you had to save yourself, you'd be in all kinds of trouble. You simply don't have the power to forgive your own sins and wash away the icky things you've done. Only God can do that!

Think about it for a minute: If you could save yourself, if you could make everything right for others, wouldn't you end up with a big head? Everyone would start saying stuff like, "Man, she's amazing!" or "Wow, she's uber-gifted!" Then what? You'd end up prideful. Puffed up. Thinking too much of yourself.

No, girl. Only God can do what only God can do. It was never up to you. That means you can rest easy and trust the work of Jesus on the cross. When He died for your sins, He covered every single one—the ones you've already committed and the ones you haven't committed yet.

He loves you that much.

Lord, I get it! I've been trying to do it all myself. I guess I think
I'm Superwoman or something. I'm always trying to fix everything!
But You're the ultimate fixer. I'm just. . .me. And I'm ready, willing,
and able to admit that I'm limited. You, though? Nothing limits You! Amen.

What Does God Say?

For we walk by faith, not by sight.
2 Corinthians 5:7 esv

You can see it. It's right in front of you. A tree was struck by lightning and it's in the middle of the road. You can't get past it. You're stuck.

Some things we see with our eyes are undeniable, like that tree. Other things? Not so much. We look at hard circumstances and we say, "That's never going to work." Or maybe we lose something important (like expensive car keys) and tell ourselves, *Give it up. You're never going to find them.*

God says something different! There really are times when you shouldn't trust your eyes (or your circumstances). He's bigger than a set of missing keys. He knows where they are, anyway.

Sure, there will be trees in the road. Avoid them. But when it comes to the other things that cause you to knee-jerk or panic? Don't be so quick to think the sky is falling. Walk by faith, girl, not by sight. Trust that God is bigger than the situation in front of you. He is, you know. He's got this.

You're bigger than the obstacles I face, Jesus. I'm so grateful! Sometimes I freeze up. I think things will never work out. Then, miraculously, they always seem to. That's only because of You. Thank You! Amen.

He's Got It All Figured Out

*Trust in the LORD with all your heart, and do not lean on
your own understanding. In all your ways acknowledge
him, and he will make straight your paths.*
PROVERBS 3:5–6 ESV

Have you ever thought you had something all figured out, only to discover you didn't? Maybe you thought you knew someone really, really well. Then they disappointed you or turned on you. Maybe they acted out in a way that totally shocked you because it went against their character or who you knew them to be.

You'll never figure out all the people and situations in this life. There are too many unknown variables! And you're not God. You can't see all things. (He can see into the hearts and minds of everyone on the planet, and all at the same time. Wow!)

Here's some good news that should help: when you place your trust in God, when you say, "Okay, I give up. I'll never figure this out on my own," you give Him the freedom to straighten out your paths. As long as your hands are on the reins, you're stuck in place. But pass those reins to Him and watch Him work on your behalf!

Trust Him, even when your situation doesn't make sense. You don't have it all figured out, but He does—and He's totally trustworthy!

*When things don't make sense, I'm so glad You have it all
figured out, Jesus. I trust You to handle all of it! Amen.*

God's Gift to You, His Child

For by grace you have been saved through faith.
And this is not your own doing; it is the gift of God.
EPHESIANS 2:8 ESV

You can't save yourself, girl. No matter how hard you try, you can't do it. And those mountains looming in front of you? Without faith, it's impossible to knock them down.

In all honesty, you would be nothing without God. He's the breath in your lungs. He's the power behind your actions. He's the driving force behind every good thing you say and do. He's the forgiver of all your sins, the Savior of your very soul. And He completely adores you—in spite of any mess-ups or flaws!

It's by His grace that you're saved. The work of Jesus on the cross changed absolutely everything. If He hadn't died for you, then you would be powerless against the enemy of your soul. But He did die. . .and He rose again, victorious! Because He triumphed over sin and the grave, you can triumph too!

This is the gift of God for you, His child! So what are you waiting for? Get out there and move some mountains, girl! You have so many amazing things to do for the kingdom of God!

I'm expecting big things, Jesus! You've given me the power
to speak to mountains, and I'm taking that task very
seriously! I'll knock them all down with Your help! Amen.

Scripture Index

OLD TESTAMENT

NEW TESTAMENT